POVERTY
ROW

POVERTY ROW

by
Gene Fernett

Library of Congress #73-86757
ISBN 0-914042-01-7

Coral Reef Publications, Inc.
Satellite Beach, FL 32937

Printed in the United States of America
1st Printing - Rose Printing Co.

Typesetting & Pagination—Cody
Publications, Inc.

Artwork by Janice Rae DeWitt

DEDICATION

To Hollywood producer Edward Finney, who suggested this volume, and whose own film productions throughout the years suggested action screen fare at its best!

ABOUT THE TITLE OF THIS BOOK

The designation of POVERTY ROW is not accepted by all persons within the film industry as a means of denoting all the studios, firms and film makers covered in this book. For example, Spencer Gordon Bennet, the great film director, says he thinks only of such firms as the Weiss Brothers and a few others, in connection with the designation.

But if one had asked a producer at one of the major film studios of the 1930's or 1940's where Poverty Row was, the chances are that he'd include within its boundaries most, if not all, the people and firms embraced in this book.

POVERTY ROW, after all, is not a single geographical area within Hollywood. As such, it defies exact definition.

ACKNOWLEDGEMENTS

Few books ever written are the products of only the authors whose names appear on them. This work is no exception. In this case, additionally, the persons who assisted the author, contributed more than they ever realized, for the author, felled by a near-fatal stroke which left him half-paralyzed, could not have undertaken this book had it not been for those whose names appear in this section and those who assisted and are not listed.

• **JACK JARDINE** . . . an enthusiastic film buff whose priceless and immense collection of motion pictures and advertising for films yielded many photographs seen in this work;

• **CARL N. BREWSTER** . . . Technicolor Corporation, who proofread this manuscript, and gave the author so much encouragement during the preparation of this work;

• **ERWIN DUMBRILLE** . . . a long time friend of the author's who carried out many of the interviews, literally wrote one chapter of the present work, and offered many suggestions that are found herein;

• **JANUS BARFOED** . . . the Danish film historian who so kindly supplied a large number of the photographs for this volume;

• **EDWARD FINNEY** . . . who contributed much to the chapters covering Grand National and Monogram.

• **SPENCER GORDON BENNET** . . . who patiently worked with the author, enlightening him with much information which made its way into these pages;

• **JOHN A. STRANSKY** and **TERRY KELLUM** . . . two of Hollywood's sound engineers who helped give the movies their voice, and the author to gain a more clear perspective of independent film production;

• **THE MITCHELL CAMERA COMPANY** . . . and the famed **MOVIOLA** firm, both Hollywood organizations whose film production devices, are an integral part of all worthwhile film production activities;

• **TECHNICOLOR INC** . . . RICHARD BLANCO, FRED DETMERS, ROBERT FORSTER and HOWARD SPRINGATE, who assisted the author in obtaining certain photographs used herein;

• **DAVID SHARPE** . . . the talented stuntman-actor who graciously supplied much for the present work;

• **MAURICE J. WILSON** . . . Director, Grand National Film Distributors, Ltd., of London, for information he supplied for use in the section on Grand National.

• **MARILYN MARLOWE** . . . who gave valuable assistance to the author.

• **TED LYDECKER** . . . who gave countless hours to interviews regarding miniatures.

To the foregoing, and to the dozens of others who lent their assistance and support to the author, sincerest thanks.

TABLE OF CONTENTS

FOREWORD

Since this book concentrates upon the two decades from 1930 to 1950, dealing with many of the small independent studios in and about Hollywood, it will cause the reader to recall a golden era of film-making, when big "major" studios each turned out fifty or sixty films a year, and small units were producing many features and serials, as well.

I recall the '30s and '40s as a trying time, particularly for film directors who were making pictures for independent production units, since that was where I did so much work. Working with low budgets, short schedules, and harried producers, the independent film director was really caught in the middle! He had to know how to "cut his picture in the camera," for example, in order to reduce laboratory costs, and to conserve film. He had to use inexpensive, yet capable, players in order to cut down the number of takes, too. My serial experience qualified me to overcome such problems, and more besides; for instance, I made the mistake of always bringing my pictures in on time, just because I thought it proper to do so. Unfortunately, producers came to take advantage of this, shortening schedules on my films to where it was practically impossible to produce a product which did not suffer as a result. But like most personnel at the independent units, I tried. All in all, they were colorful days, and their problems do not make me less proud to have been a part of that era, when we turned out pictures that were clean and entertaining.

Spencer Gordon Bennet
Hollywood, California

Where Did it All Begin?

THE Poverty Row history has no clear-cut beginning, simply because many motion picture studios which eventually became major firms often themselves were of the kind of beginnings that typify a Poverty Row organization. But by 1930, a circle of affluent film producers had emerged in Hollywood, separating themselves from the small independent firms which were eventually to be known as "the cowpokes of Gower Gulch." Then did Poverty Row have an identity and a Hollywood address.

For prior to World War I, American film makers were scattered across the country. The famous old-Selig Polyscope firm, once made its headquarters in Chicago, as did the Essanay outfit. The Edison firm centered its film making enterprise around Camden, New Jersey, while the Biograph outfit headquartered in New York City, along with J. Stuart Blackton's "rooftop studio." A lot of the pioneer firms centered their activities around Fort Lee, New Jersey, or Astoria, Long Island. A few of them operated out of Florida and other "remote" areas. It was a period of extreme decentralization, and a time when the motion picture was a mere novelty, in many cases being only an "act" within a vaudeville program.

In short, the film industry was a modest enterprise prior to the time World War I, its fortunes but modest ones. It was an industry which probably was not even known to Mrs. H. H. Wilcox, the wife of an early real estate promoter in California, who, in the mid-1880's, named a small area north of Los Angeles "Hollywood," after the summer place of an old friend who lived in Chicago.

In 1907, early film makers had discovered that the little community of Hollywood possessed an ideal climate for their picture making, as Colonel William Selig demonstrated in 1909 when he produced the first entirely made-in-Hollywood film. His good judgment was verified in 1910, when David Horsley leased the northwest corner of Sunset Boulevard and Gower Street and there erected a primitive but serviceable studio for the Nestor Company. Producer D. W. Griffith had already found that Hollywood offered an ideal location, and provided a welter of nearby locations, too. The uncanny foresight of these pioneers was attested to by the legions of later film makers who came to Hollywood, not the least of whom became the dwellers of the town's "Poverty Row."

After World War I, the film gradually became a widely recognized art form, with the result that the film makers began to separate themselves — by design or accident — into distinctly separate groups. One group made films which aspired to artistic, impressive and memorable presentations. The films of some of this group are today preserved in "film museums" — the likes of Charles Chaplin, Mary Pickford, D. W. Griffith, and so on. Still another group sought only to make entertainment, usually with no pretense to perma-

1

nence. Often, such film makers had good budgets, and could be relatively lavish in production of such pictures as they chose to make. A third group made no pretense of turning out artistic productions. Using second-string players, writers and crews, they sought only to produce films (often of an action nature) which would return a profit. It is this third group which were the forerunners of the production outfits which, in the era of talking pictures, made up the populace of Poverty Row.

Gower Gulch film making activity, it should be noted, moved toward its zenith when "talkies" became a permanent film expression back in the late 1920's. It was an odd, inappropriate time to pan for gold really, because there was the world-wide economic slump to discourage the entrepreneurs of such enterprises, not to mention the expense of sound pictures, which required more equipment and personnel than had the earlier voiceless films.

Some little production outfits did not succeed, it's true, for the simple reason that there were so many such organizations in Hollywood. In fact, a roll call of those firms which went out of existence during the decade would serve perhaps to point up how the first years of sound pictures were an age of high mortality on Poverty Row. There were Big Four Pictures, Dick Talmadge Productions, Showmen's Pictures, Action Pictures, Cameo Pictures, World Wide and Mayfair Pictures Corporation, who were just a few of the fatalities of that first decade. But in their wake they left many survivors, including Puritan, Commodore, Burroughs-Tarzan, B. F. Zeidman, Mascot, Chesterfield, Ambassador-Conn, Liberty, Republic, Empire, George Hirliman Enterprises, Monogram, Supreme, Syndicate, Stage and Screen, Spectrum, Victory, Regal

and Invincible. All of the latter were very active in the period which began in 1935, and a handful of them lasted a decade or more afterward.

With such a welter of names actively competing with the major studios, it is little wonder that they were seldom taken seriously by the "majors" and thus were free to develop for themselves players, personnel and film series, which they quite often made into profitable entities.

By the onset of World War II, Hollywood's film production centers were more stabilized than before, the small independent outfits largely eliminated from the scene, or else releasing their films through one of the labels which, while operating outside that select circle of eight major studios, helped keep the motion picture theatres outside of the "Axis Nations" well supplied with pictures.

In those busy war years, Hollywood pumped out as many as 600 feature length productions. Such immense output produced many shabby, unimaginative pictures — both from independent producers and major studios — many of which television audiences of recent years have shaken their heads and chuckled to see again. But the same period produced some rightfully memorable features, many of which can be viewed even now with zeal and appreciation. Within this admirable circle of motion pictures are numerous films which were made down on Poverty Row, and which hold their own kind of timeless magic.

Viewed today, many of Poverty Row offerings of the period with which this book concerns itself — 1930 through 1950 — are yet worthy of one's time to study and to marvel at. Most do not reach the artistic heights of those films made at major studios during the same period, but the best of them are examples of independent film production at its very best. As such, some of these films are worthy not only of casual examination, but of preservation by such film libraries as the Museum of Modern Art. Such films are, after all, a large segment of American film history.

Dreamland Theatre (*Saginaw, Michigan*), *which perished fairly early in the sound picture era, but was a favorite of movie goers who didn't have much to spend on entertainment.*

The American Movie Theatres: 1930 — 1950

IN order to completely understand the phenomenon of Poverty Row and its sizeable population during the period 1930-1950, it is necessary to consider the overall size of the film industry at that time.

This era with which we are concerned, covered an estimated weekly world-wide market potential of some two hundred million people — about seventy-five million of them attending twelve thousand theatres in the United States alone. So, to serve such a huge audience, Hollywood was annually paying out seventy-five million dollars in salaries back in the 1930's!

The productions thus generated, went forth to a variety of theatres, including austere downtown film palaces — those mausoleum-like structures which housed literally armies of uniformed ushers — and to the strangely anachronistic and invariably dingy side-street theatres which were politely called "subsequent run" theatres, but which were popularly termed "shooting gallery houses" because many were of the long and narrow room variety.

This curiously diverse array of movie houses was the marketplace for all that Hollywood had to offer; its celluloid shadows being presented by machinery

The small independent studios of Hollywood vied with the large, major ones to provide the "stock in trade" of such theatres as this one in London, England. Here, like everywhere in the movie-going world, Saturday matinee crowds demanded motion picture thrills of the type that "Poverty Row" could mete out in quantity! [Photo courtesy of Harold W. Seacombe]

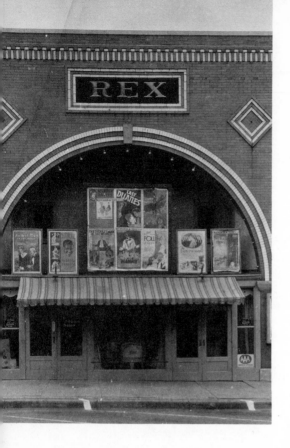

which in many cases dated back to World War I — and some even earlier — and the later attachment of cumbersome sound devices which had to be made when the sound picture craze overtook the cinema and thrilled the public.

The "shooting gallery" theatre, the small-town cinema, the little theatre, all catered to less than sophisticated audiences who were the prime customers for the films turned out by the studios of Poverty Row. The success of these small theatres was vital to the producer who lived by making such films as the western, the serial, and the pictures which fell generally in the "B" picture category, particularly those of an action or a light comedy nature. To these productions, the owner of the

American counterparts of the countless foreign theatres which ran the films of the small Hollywood independent producer were the Caldwell Theatre, St. Joseph, Michigan, and the Rex Theatre, Three Rivers, Michigan. Generations of action lovers chomped many tons of popcorn while watching Jack Hoxie, Bob Steele, Gene Autry and Eddie Dean at theatres such as these. [Both photos courtesy of Lyle W. Smith/W. S. Butterfield Theatres, Inc.]

small theatre* invariably added the glossy prestige of the "subsequent run" of major pictures — often third or fourth run behind the large downtown cinema houses.

The small theatre was in many ways a poor and dilapidated cousin of its downtown namesake, but it was a segment of cinema history which is deserving of more attention than it has received. It was, after all, the reason for the existence of all of Hollywood's Poverty Row area, the device by which countless persons saw most, if not all, movies of the time.

From cramped, uncomfortable, concrete-and-asbestos projection booths, these shabby little theatres poured forth a flickering array of images, creating a dream world for countless thousands of persons the world over.

In what often had once been a grocery store, a pair of antique Powers Model 6-B projection machines ground away at the thousands of feet of film that the place presented its customers, and to the sound of which film patrons busily chomped thousands of paper sacks of popcorn each year.

It was part of screen history's nitrate film era, the 35mm stock being a form of gun cotton, demanding fire precautions little needed nowadays, regardless of the size of the theatre.

In the era covered by this book, the prestigious "down town theatres" usually held to a single feature policy, rounding out such programs with one or more short subjects and often

including newsreel.

"Subsequent run" houses, on the other hand, seemed most profitable when they presented double features — often during the depression years accompanied by "Bingo Nights", "Bank Nights" or similar promotions. Typical change of weekly programs at such houses might offer one bill on Sunday and Monday, followed by Tuesday, Wednesday and Thursday program feature, with still another change of bill on Friday and Saturday. In other words, there were three complete program changes each week at many "subsequent run" theatres, calling for more than three hundred features per year, in part explaining the immense output of Hollywood at that time.

What is amazing is that this vast film market had existed for decades prior to the coming of the talking pictures and stimulated the growth of a coterie of independent production firms.

However, in the early days of film making, it was more difficult to identify which studio was a shoestring operation and which was a well-financed one. Such early firms as Edison operated a film production unit which was never a large scale operation and which therefore was quite similar to the small independents.

By 1930, however, few of the firms of the silent film era still existed, small or large. Gone completely were such firms as American Film Company, Jewel, Butterfly, Arrow Film Company, Selig, Biograph and others which had existed during the period of World War I and immediately just afterwards.

A new roll call of firms came into being with few of the names directly

---

*Theatres of this nature were earliest hit by the coming of television.

linked with the World War I era in evidence — Universal and a few others being exceptions.

Most were relatively newcomers, and they sought to establish themselves as dependable production centers for some of the world's thousands of theatres which, newly equipped for sound pictures, needed more and more films, it seemed, with each passing week.

Into the Side Streets

"**O**UR real job was not making our films," one Gower Gulch alumnus explained, "it was the task of getting our pictures into all the side street theatres of the nation."

To accomplish that end, the small independent producer established his own network of "film exchanges" if he had sufficient output to supply them year around; or entrusted distribution to outlets which represented several producers, if he didn't — usually licensing the "states' right" distributors for periods of five years.

Republic, Mascot, Grand National, Monogram, PRC and a handful of other film outfits (aside from the large "major" studios) were able to maintain their own networks of exchanges, sometimes in the cases of non-majors, merely "franchising" them to distribute throughout a given area, or "states' right" the films as specified by the producer.*

One of the interesting sidelights of this phase of motion picture activity is that several terms still in use came down from the late 1890's and early 1900's. For example, the practice of renting films to theatres is to this day referred to as "buying" films — in deference to the old practice of literally buying a film for a theatre to show, then exchanging the film for something else. In fact, the term

"film exchange" stems also from the early days of motion pictures, when exhibitors "exchanged" prints after their theatre had played them, and got something they had not played.

From the early days, a pattern of cities became established, strategically located geographically so that no U.S. theatre would be more than a few hundred miles from a "film center" and so could receive prints (usually by a special truck line which specialized in delivery of film) in just a few hours time.

As this type of distribution chain was gradually manifesting itself, the many "poster exchanges" were grouping themselves, usually in or near cities which also were film distribution centers.

In the East and South, film exchanges were centered in cities such as New York, Buffalo, Memphis and Atlanta. In the West, similar "exchange areas" were to be found in cities such as Salt Lake City, Portland (Oregon), Los Angeles, and others.

Whenever American productions were shipped abroad, another network of distributors was added. For the Poverty Row film organization — except in large concentrated markets such as England — distribution was difficult. However, firms such as Trans-Oceanic Film Export Company (with offices in New York, London, Paris and Madrid) undertook foreign distribution for many independent producers of Hollywood.

---

*We have a modern day counterpart in the franchised operation of many restaurants, motels, etc.

In some areas of the English-speaking world, distribution of independent films from Hollywood was quite simple if handled by a relatively large distribution chain, such as Ritchie Import, or the Canadian outlet, Empire Film Distributors. In both cases, the firms had rather widespread distribution through a network of offices, and maintained separate "prints" of each production in every exchange center.

Hollywood producers, it should be stressed, did not usually purchase from their film laboratories the prints of their pictures which were assigned to various distributors. Where a producer assigned "states right" terms, these called for the exchanges themselves to purchase the prints (copies) of each picture struck from the negatives which the producer himself controlled. By this means, Poverty Row was able to confine its cash outlay to producing the film and to preparing only those "screening prints" which each producer required for his own use, leaving the costs of producing prints for use within the theatres to distributors themselves.

While the pictures of Hollywood studios were the leading films of the world at that time, no American film executive of the 1930's and 1940's would deny the competitive existence of other film production centers throughout the world, particularly those of England. Names such as Twickenham, B.I.P., London Films, Gaumont-British and others gave evidence that the British not only could make pictures which had a world-wide appeal, but were quite profitable as U.S. imports, some of which American firms were proud to distribute under their trademarks. Of the independent studios in Hollywood, Edward R. Alperson's Grand National Firm was notable for its British offerings. Some of the Grand National releases

from England, for example, included the prestige feature *Moonlight Sonata,* (the only film in which the pianist Paderewski appeared), the pleasant adventure *Hideout In The Alps* and the Boris Karloff picture *Juggernaut.*

An entirely different approach to placing foreign films within view of American audiences was assayed by a New York distribution firm called DuWorld Films. Like several other companies of the time, DuWorld operated much like an independent film exchange serving Poverty Row, except that it derived most of its product from foreign producers, as in part did J. H. Hoffberg and Amity Pictures.

Distributors, foreign film labels and producers who turned out entertainment films under an impressive-sounding "studio name" but released under the name of some other firm, all were common in the decade of the 1930's but were less in evidence by the time of World War II.

Broadway Productions, Campbell Productions, Inspiration Pictures, Select Pictures, Cosmopolitan, Gotham and a few other outfits were based in the East, principally around New York City, where they found time to grind out pictures that many film lovers swore they could detect from those that Hollywood was offering concurrently. They offered, nonetheless, a degree of competition which was somewhat comparable to the influx of foreign films, offering a recognizable but weak competitive force against Hollywood's films.

It should be borne in mind that entertainment films of the '30s and '40s were rented to theatres in one of two distinctly different fashions. The first, and then the most common rental method, involved a flat rental, the rate itself based upon the size of the theatre, its location, and whether the customer was playing pictures first run, second run, etc. The second method employed was to contract for each showing on a percentage basis; theatres involved in such a rental plan were subject to "spot checking" by agents of the film distribution office, of course. The percentage charged by producers was initially as low as 15% of the gross at the box-office, but this figure eventually reached 50% and 60% by the time World War II ended.

For the producers of Poverty Row status, however, "straight rentals" usually have been the rule; moreover, in the period covered in this volume, such was the standard practice for virtually all "independent films." Rental rates during even this period were extremely variable, with some small sidestreet motion picture houses paying only about ten dollars for a feature, and as low as a dollar or two for a one reel short subject.

Such rentals could not produce any phenomenal income for the film producer whose sign was emblazoned on some door which opened onto "Gower Gulch".

Still the profits to be derived from "shoestring" film production were in line with other American profits of small firms of that era. The 1930's were part of that gloomy period called the "great depression." Everything, not just film rentals and theatre admissions, was low. The famed Park Central Hotel in New York City was advertising suites of rooms at only five dollars a day, while a competitor, the Hotel Edison, was trumpeting rates of two dollars and a half. Plainly, the dollar bought a great deal then!

Later, in spite of the economic effect of World War II, film rentals remained relatively low. It was a happy time for theatre owners, who watched the wartime crowds line up at the box offices, helping producers to increase domestic film rentals, and thus offset losses of so many overseas outlets.

American film exchanges were tremendously active during these war years and that activity was in turn reflected on Hollywood, whose major film producers and independent film makers were happily "cashing in." It was a period when virtually everyone in the film business was profiting, in production, exhibition, and of course, in distribution.

At least as far as domestic distribution was concerned, the war years were golden ones, indeed. And for that area of global distribution which remained open to U. S. producers, the profits were constant and sizeable.

Poverty Row — or what remained of it by World War II — cut itself in on a share of the wartime bonanza.

A moment's pause during the production of an early "talkie" at one of the sound stages of Tiffany Pictures. (Photo courtesy of John A. Stransky, Jr.)

Of Men and Machines:
The Production Gear

EVEN though the coming of sound made the business of film making more complex, expensive and time consuming, it still was no Herculean task to get into production, thanks to the plethora of equipment, men and supplies which were available at daily or weekly rates to any film producer who could prove reasonable financial resources.

Such producers had available to them, for example, a large number of rental stages — Tec-Art, Larry Darmour, General Services Studios, and others. There was plenty of camera equipment available, too, either at the sound stages, or from outfits such as Hollywood Camera Exchange or Mark Armistead. Similarly, sound equipment — even crews to go with such gear — was available from International Sound Recording, Disney Recording Company, and scores of others.

Rentals often were used to augment the smaller, lighter equipment which some small firm production outfits owned. Most of the Poverty Row dwellers did not go beyond certain basic equipment, however.

Obviously, the major film studios owned much of their equipment, sets, costumes and so forth. The small, independent producer more frequently rented or borrowed that which he needed for a picture, and to him the "rental agencies" were lifeblood.

When one small-time producer was filming a picture about the Everglades, Charles T. O'Rork — who was chief cameraman on that film — recalled that the script called for a full-scale hurricane to be photographed on a sound stage. Reputedly for a case of beer, the producer borrowed an air boat and a steel dump truck. Then, with the powerful fan on the air boat to throw the "rain" and the steel dump truck to hold the water necessary for the scene, a mighty convincing hurricane was made to order — at Poverty Row production rates! This anecdote illustrates how "big scenes" often were possible for "shoestring" producers whose personnel possessed limited budgets, but unlimited imagination!

All manner of agencies aided the independent producer. Not even the casting of a film needed to be accomplished by the producer, who could, if he chose, hire that chore performed by one of Hollywood's several agencies who specialized in casting for studios down on Poverty Row.

Even the most lavish costume drama was possible for the smaller producer, thanks to costume rentals from firms such as Western Costume Corporation, The Oriental Costume Company and others. Of these firms, one of them, Western Costume, now boasts a multi-million dollar wardrobe of historically documented clothes, as well as a library of 80,000 volumes which its customers

This is the world's largest costumers — Western Costume Company, as the plant and showrooms appeared during the era covered by this volume. Still one of the leading costume suppliers to film production and TV producers alike, the firm was also a major supplier to the many independent film makers who once dwelt along the mythical "Poverty Row".

A part of the vast collection of clothes — in total, said to be a million costumes — available from Western Costume Company, Hollywood. [Photo courtesy of Western Costume Company]

14

may refer to before filming any picture which requires historically correct costuming.

If the producer was working on a restricted budget but nonetheless wished to make a busy and action-filled western, he need not worry; plenty of extras in cowboy garb could be hired for as little as five dollars a day (during the depression). Horses were easily obtained and at ridiculously low prices at places such as Jones Riding Stables or Iverson's Ranch.

One of the facts about independent film production which often has not been made clear in recounting film history is that so-called "Poverty Row" film units utilized exactly the same makes of production gear as the "major" studios were using during the same period. Mitchell (or Bell and Howell) cameras, Moviola editing gear, Mole-Richardson lighting units, RCA and Western Electric recording machines all were standard for small and large film units. Such equipment,

whether rented or purchased, was capable of producing motion pictures which, mechanically and electronically, were of pleasing quality. The difference then, of independent productions most often was that of what was filmed, not the equipment used in the production.

The similarity between major production and independent ones did not hold true where color pictures were concerned, though. In fact, only Tiffany, which produced some film in the early two-strip type Technicolor, and Republic which, in the latter days of its history, offered some features in the standard three-strip Technicolor, were about the only small independent studios to dabble in any really acceptable color process. The other independents invariably offered colored pictures which used one of the primitive chromatic methods, such as Cinecolor, Magnacolor, or Trucolor.

Of the many processes to achieve a measure of prominence, which included Kinecolor, Brewster Color, Dufaycolor,

Here is one of the more complex models of the famous Moviola editing equipment, in this case, one which will project a picture from one strip of film, while "playing back" four sound tracks simultaneously. [Photo courtesy of Moviola]

The Cinecolor offices and processing plant in North Hollywood. In the period from 1930 to 1950 alone, Cinecolor turned out thousands of feet of inexpensive color prints for many producers of independent pictures, thus providing a low-cost — if far inferior — substitute for the genuine three-strip Technicolor product. [Photo courtesy of Erwin Dumbrille]

Sennett Color, and literally dozens of others, the one in greatest popularity was the Cinecolor system, derived from a slightly earlier method called Multicolor. Both were developed by an English-born inventor, William Thomas Crespinel, who launched Cinecolor commercially in early 1932 at a plant located at 201 Occidental Boulevard, Hollywood.

The Cinecolor system was attractive to small producers because of its low cost, which was only about 25% above that of ordinary black and white film. Besides this cost advantage, Cinecolor needed only Mitchell or Bell and Howell cameras, slightly modified to accommodate two strips of negative, which passed through the camera face to face.

However, Cinecolor not only did not provide a true rendition of the color spectrum, but in projection was always partially out of focus, since the release prints involved printing colors on both sides of the base of the film stock used. Nonetheless, Cinecolor — and the later, more impressive Super Cinecolor (1952) — was capable of producing more than acceptable results when judiciously handled.

While many major producers, including M-G-M, Columbia, Universal, United Artists, RKO, and 20th Century-Fox, made some releases in Cinecolor,* the biggest usage of the process oc-

*The release of PRC's feature *Enchanted Forest* (1945) is said to have spurred much of the "major" studios interest in Cinecolor.

This is the early Technicolor two-color system. A beam-splitting prism and filters were used to produce images on two strips of black-and-white film. Tiffany Productions used such a camera in producing the feature, **Mamba**. They were among the only "Poverty Row" firms to engage the Technicolor device. [Photo courtesy of Technicolor and Messrs. Fred Detmers and Richard Blanco]

This is an honored 35mm camera from the renowned Mitchell Camera Corporation of Hollywood. In the 1930s and 40s this particular model, the NC, was one of the most popular in virtually all of the professional firms, from the Poverty Row outfits to the large, major studios. [Photo courtesy of Mitchell Camera Corp.]

Mitchell 35mm
Sound Model (NC)
Camera

curred along Poverty Row. In fact, it was Monogram who released the earliest Cinecolor offering and, ironically, the successor to Monogram (Allied Artists) which made the final Cinecolor feature in 1955. The process was most popular immediately after World War II, when many low and medium budget features were produced in Cinecolor, including independent features made by Monogram, Republic, PRC, and Screen Guild.

The deficiencies posed by primitive color films were the primary photographic weakness of the output of pictures made by the small independent film producer. The cameraman who worked along Poverty Row probably shrugged this off as he did the usual lack of large camera booms and other complex devices, such as that of sophisticated lighting equipment.

Men such as Archie Stout, Ernest Miller and others turned in serviceable, sometimes imaginative photographic jobs for producers of independent releases, in spite of such limitations.

The photography and lighting constituted only parts of the technical phases of the motion picture, however. When the talking picture became an accepted device with the film-going public, the sound engineer became an integral part of Hollywood's technicians. Using equipment and experience developed primarily by early radio, these men were able to adapt the devices to the talking picture. Even sound effects gadgets were transferred to Hollywood from the radio studio — not from the techniques of the stage, as were the lighting equipment found

throughout early Hollywood.

The sound equipment which pioneer engineers in Hollywood "borrowed" from radio stations was changed in its functions and its applications when it was adapted for the talking picture, as when the microphones were placed out of sight of the cameras, and thus were forced to amplify sounds far more than most radio engineers generally were called upon to do.

Often, nothing but simple "sunlight reflectors" were used outdoors, with none of the heavy electrical equipment that so many major studios used as "fill light" on exteriors. The down-at-the-heels independents seldom added such devices as complex camera cranes either, for these required time to utilize properly, and greater budgetary requirements in any production in which they were used. Simple camera gear such as a standard tripod was the rule. And surprisingly, the productions so made, did not suffer a great deal from the lack of artistry so engendered in them.

These differences aside, most of Hollywood's early sound equipment was merely commercial gear of the type used by radio networks and individual stations. To this equipment, design engineers added film recording devices, such as early types of variable area or else the variable density system of recording sound, both of which recorded directly onto film. Occasionally, in the 1920's, they accomplished the miracle of sound recording by coupling heavy, cumbersome gear which preserved sounds on giant 16-inch discs, such as Warner Brothers used in its early sound films — the Vitaphone process, as Warners called it. Mercifully, the old "sound on disc" method died in the early 1930's, leaving only "sound on film" types, all of which were interchangeable as far as their use in theatres.

It was not until the postwar era that any new type sound recording came to be introduced. At that time magnetic recording was developed, largely from devices first used in Germany during World War II. This methodology came to America and the film making scene about the same time that television made its inroads. It was, in reality, a development which came too late to serve much of "Poverty Row."

The editors of *American Cinematographer* magazine recently stated that early sound pictures required eight tons of equipment in order to accomplish "location shooting". What was surprising about such an immense quantity of gear was that it produced sound of such limited quality, that it never approached the standards of today's home tape recorders!

By 1950, however, — when our present foray into film history ends — magnetic recording devices had replaced the optical sound recorder, and the weight of recording gear was already down to fifty pounds or so. (Presently, pocket recorders have been developed which are transistorized and which require only common cassettes of tapes to record high quality motion picture sound).

It should be borne in mind that Hollywood's post-1930's history is fraught with examples of the adaptation or modification of equipment either made for another market, or else made for use in producing silent pictures, as were virtually all the cameras utilized in turning out the early talking films.

In the early months of the talking picture boom, even the simplest of specialized devices which would become associated with the sound film industry, were not commercially available, such as the "microphone boom." Instead, broadcast types of microphones were "spotted" about motion picture sets, often suspended from above by ropes! John A. Stransky, Jr., who was a recording engineer at Tiffany Studios in the opening days of the sound film goldrush, described to this author the first "mike booms":

"We nailed together crude, overhead movable arms, made from 2 x 4's and counter-balanced by sandbags. These permitted us, after a fashion, to follow actors as they moved about the set, recording sound. These rough gadgets eventually led manufacturers to design the mike booms which came into use."

Ingenious men and novel machines. Together, they made possible the miracle which was the talking picture, thus helping all of Hollywood to keep working throughout the great economic recession which struck our nation in the late 1920's and all of the 1930's. More cogent to the present story, they made feasible the continuance of Poverty Row.

Small World, Isn't It

THE deceptive business of utilizing miniatures in motion pictures has long been a mainstay of all commercial film production. Early in film history, for instance, miniatures were employed by film makers to simulate the battle between Spanish and U. S. warships involved in action around Cuba during the Spanish-American War.*

During the talking picture era, the art of the miniature and the photography of such sets came into breathtaking realism, molded by the skilled hands of such men as Theodore and Howard Lydecker, William Davison and Ray Harryhausen, the latter of whom created the effects in *King Kong*.

Miniatures, which may range from very minute objects up to some which approach the real thing they seek to emulate, are most effective in the motion picture when used in short scenes, which utilize — when possible — the largest, most detailed models, which can simulate the real object with such remarkable detail that they are virtually indistinguishable.

A high degree of illusion was achieved in several miniatures used in the early Mascot talkie serials,* but as an art reached its peak of deceptive success at the hands of Theodore and Howard Lydecker, who produced startlingly real-appearing miniaturizations used in the Republic serials, particularly prior to 1950, when the overall cost of such sequences was relatively reasonable, and more or less ambitious miniatures possible.

It should be borne in mind that virtually all motion picture sequences of naval encounters, as well as "submarine" scenes are the results of miniatures. At their most convincing, the surface scenes may involve the use of small "ships" which are large enough to house a man to operate the vessel, and are photographed in a swimming-pool sized tank, behind which a suitable and undistracting background is suspended or projected — sometimes by superimpose — or on a lake or ocean, as budgets may allow.

The creators of these illusions work with almost all devices, all art media. Some miniatures work out so well that the human eye simply cannot distinguish the fakery. At other screen moments, the deception is quite clear, as in the famed motion picture, *King Kong*.

---

*See the book, *"Two Reels and a Crank"* which details this particular use of a very crude miniature to substitute for the real scene.

---

*As in the scenes showing a gyrocopter landing on a model of the "Bekin warehouse" in Hollywood. This footage appears in the Mascot serial *The Whispering Shadow*. The gyrocopter (a forerunner of the helicopter) also was used in the Bob Steele serial made later at Mascot.

At their most spectacular, and convincing, miniatures may include sequences which involve scale models produced on several different "scales" depending upon the camera angles, perspective, and the details involved. If miniatures are to be used for lengthy sequences and are to maintain their illusion of reality, detailed, and varying scales of the models are involved.

The miniatures utilized may be as simple as a photographic enlargement which is judiciously "combined" with miniatures as may blend into a convincing overall scene. Such scenes, and other more complex sequences, are then often used in conjunction with a type of animation usually described as "stop motion" to produce an illusion of motion from a still, but manually operated, object as in the scenes for *King Kong.*

Much has been made by writers of screen history regarding the "bigness" of the screen images of these miniatures and their overall impressiveness when enlarged to theatrical proportions. A portion of such seeming size is attained from the accompanying sound track; the sound effects and the music serving to give much feeling of bigness to these miniatures. "It was up to us in the sound department to cook up these weird sounds which accompanied Ted and Howard Lydecker's miniatures," said sound engineer Terry Kellum only recently. "We amplified everyday, ordinary sounds and made of them something impressive, awesome, even frightening. Audiences overlook these 'finishing touches' to the miniature sequences, which wouldn't be half so impressive were it not for the sound track."

This model automobile appeared in the Republic serial, **Mysterious Dr. Satan** *[1940], as it plunged over a cliff. Note the rails on which the model runs, which are concealed in the motion picture sequence. [Photo courtesy of Ted Lydecker]*

What looks to be a full long shot of a real railroad, is actually a Lydecker miniature used in the Republic feature **The Great Train Robbery** [1941]. [Photo courtesy of Ted Lydecker]

A striking realistic miniature used in the Bob Steele Republic western **The Great Train Robbery** [1941]. The plot revolves about the theft of an entire railroad train and its concealment within a mountain [by means of a "spur" line from the main line, hastily laid by the criminals]. Naturally, miniatures played a big part in cinematically, making all this possible! [Photo courtesy of Ted Lydecker]

A gigantic hydroelectric plant? No, it's another Lydecker Brothers' model for use in the Republic feature, **Born to be Wild.** [Photo courtesy of Ted Lydecker]

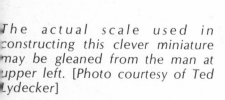

The actual scale used in constructing this clever miniature may be gleaned from the man at upper left. [Photo courtesy of Ted Lydecker]

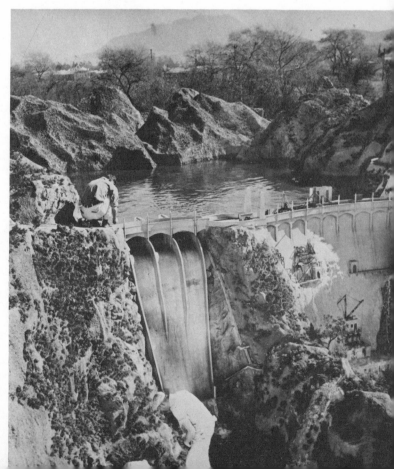

One cannot go around blowing up actual dams for the purpose of making films, so a model is constructed. The resulting explosion of this miniature creates life-like destruction. [Photo courtesy of Ted Lydecker]

The final results of the destruction of the miniature dam by the Lydeckers. [I do believe they like destroying things.]

The use of miniatures in the form of rear screen projections behind "live action" scenes (either by the device of projecting motion picture footage or "plates" — i.e. slides — of miniatures) has been frequently utilized as a means of enhancement. By such means, monsters can be created from tiny lizards, chinese dragons and the like, and then projected behind actors in order to create action-filled sequences.

The author does not wish to cast the misimpression that rear-screen projections are entirely made up of miniatures, because they are not. Nonetheless, projection of sequences which have been produced by the use of miniatures long has been a big part of Hollywood's bag of illusions. During the two decades covered by this volume, the rear screen method was the only practical system of projecting plates and motion pictures as a background for a scene. The problem of rendering a background projection so that it matched the foreground was a problem Hollywood producers large and small shared in the two decades with which we are concerned here. Such problems as the matching of camera lenses which were used to photograph the background scene with those used to capture the "composite sequence," overall lighting of the scene, similarity of film "grain structures" and other seemingly insurmountable photographic problems plagued film makers, whether they were working along Poverty Row or at MGM.

As an interesting contrast to the older rear screen system, it is interesting to note that Hollywood now possesses devices which allow the projection of plates or motion picture sequences (including continuous "loops" of film) from in front of the set, by the use of a "half-silvered" mirror which allows a camera and a projector in effect to work from identical angles, and thus to conceal the fact that actors and other foreground "obstacles" in the light are blocking a part of the projected image — i.e., are creating unwanted silhouettes on the screen in back of themselves, which are unseen by the camera only because it is matched carefully to the angle at which the projection of the background is being made, too.

With such a device unknown to early Hollywood, and thus to our Poverty Row filmers, our less than affluent producers contented themselves with a few rear screen projections, either with or without the use of these clever miniatures which we are discussing in this chapter. Such projected footage rarely was convincing, except when used judiciously, whether employing miniatures or not. Miniatures did not find widespread applications within the western films, only rarely being a part of that genre.

It was in the serials — both those produced on Poverty Row and by major studios — that the genius of the miniature maker was most often applied. After all, the multi-acre set which would have been required for a full-scale mockup of, say, Murania (the underground city in the Mascot chapter play *The Phantom Empire*) simply would not have been within the budget for such a film. So, instead, artists' renderings, and model buildings, some with animated devices, substituted effectively. Moreover, when such sequences were edited together with footage of the Muranian queen and her courtiers (in reality filmed within an observatory tower which happened to be nearing completion near Hollywood) Murania was very real, as far as the theatre audiences of 1935 were concerned.

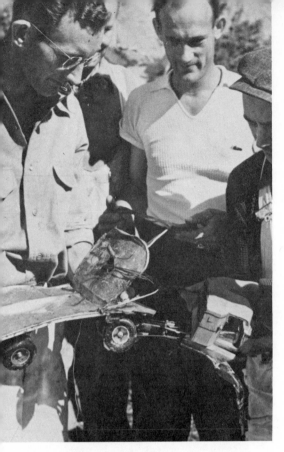

A toy truck, crossing the set at the time, is shown above. Gun powder, even when judiciously used, creates havoc. The metal miniature truck is a replica of many real ones used around Republic at the time so that models and shots of an actual truck could be "intercut" in the film. [Photo courtesy of Ted Lydecker]

When Mascot Pictures merged with Monogram and Liberty to become Republic Pictures, that merger brought together the many elements which were necessary in one way or another to a high degree of development of the miniature art.

It gave the Lydeckers — the men responsible for Republic's miniatures — better budgets than those afforded them by earlier independent film makers, and the unlimited use of optical effects at Consolidated Film Industries,* plus Republic's around-the-calendar demand for action pictures and serials. By the time that the Lydeckers undertook the manufacture of the many miniatures used in Republic pictures, the availability of numerous then new materials, processes, lenses and lighting equipment made their work more flexible, and much more "believable" than were some of the earlier such screen sequences.

Throughout the two decades we are discussing, it is important to consider just how many seemingly "big scenes," thrilling moments which the art of the miniature made possible. And for the producer along Poverty Row, film deception by the use of miniatures literally made possible scenes which otherwise could not have been shown.

"The funny thing about Republic serials," said Ted Lydecker recently, "was how frequently they depended upon miniatures for those big moments that led up to exciting conclusions for various chapters. Think about it for a moment; explosions, floods, ships in peril, and yes, even cars going over cliffs. Almost all were miniatures which my brother Howard and I fashioned."

---

*Herbert J. Yates, who controlled Republic also operated the Consolidated Film operation.

The role of miniatures assumed the proportions it reached at Republic Studios through a period of gradual evolution. As Ted Lydecker explained it, "We were working in a sort of shoe box at Mascot, during the last days, then readying the serial *Undersea Kingdom*. Jack Coile was at that time in charge of the carpenter shop — and the prop shop. He wasn't there too long, and my brother took over.

"We quickly outgrew the little shack we were working in, so we moved to larger quarters, a shop on the back lot at Republic. There, a crew of about 15 or 20 men turned out our miniatures.

"In our work, we developed various scales of size, usually three-fourths inch to the foot, sometimes one inch to the foot. These are scales which we arrived at after working with our father, Howard Lydecker, Senior, who, as you

The scene is from Republic's color feature of 1953, **Fair Wind To Java,** *starring Fred MacMurray and Vera Ralston. Although the film does not fall within the limits of 1930-1950, as implied by this book's subtitle, it is included pictorially for this scene, is a spectacular Lydecker miniature, photographed on Lake Mono, California. The ship model, in reality, is something over twelve feet long, and houses a man who steers the craft for the scene. Propulsive power is by underwater cable. [Photo courtesy of Ted Lydecker]*

This is the crew required for producing only the miniatures used in the John Wayne/Republic offering **Flying Tigers.** The workers are [first row] Champagne, Lincoff, Olson, Cottle, Day and Moody; [second row] Hughes, Al Edens, Chambers, and Svedeen; [back row] unidentified, Bill Bradford, Shorty Stafford, Howard "Babe" Lydecker, unidentified, Ted Lydecker, unidentified. Note the excellent cloud formations overhead, which discloses why the Lydeckers chose to film all the airplane scenes here, at Sante Fe, New Mexico. All miniatures were utilized in this flying film. [Photo and identification by courtesy of Ted Lydecker]

According to Ted Lydecker who, with his late brother Howard, made the marvelous miniatures used in all Republic films, there were no actual planes in the John Wayne feature **The Flying Tigers** [1942]. Even the Air Corps experts were fooled by the Lydeckers' deception!

know, did so much set design and building 'way back in the silent days — for Douglas Fairbanks, Charlie Ray and the like.''

''My brother Howard and I stayed at Republic from the start of that organization to its finish, when Republic was doing films such as *Quiet Man,* and so on. Together, we were a team, you see — the Lydecker twins, people often called us. We weren't twins, though. Actually I was three years older than Howard.''

''But we didn't mind being called twins. We were very close to each other, working alongside each other at Republic, fishing buddies and near neighbors out in North Hollywood.''

''Few people outside the film industry even were aware of all the miniatures they were viewing. And I'm sure they didn't know the 'Lydecker twins' were working together making that small, detailed world seem so huge.''

Small Gems From Tiffany

ONE OF Hollywood's studios which now is all but forgotten by the public is Tiffany Pictures, a firm whose history began in the late silent picture period and extended until the early sound film era. Tiffany's history includes a noteworthy list of feature productions and a smattering of short subjects, as well.

During the silent era, the company released its products through major film labels. In the "talkie film" period, however, its products were offered through a world-wide network of independent film distributors, thus marking Tiffany as a Poverty Row producer, as defined by this book.

In 1926, the firm issued a leatherette-bound "Tiffany Art Album," trumpeting its early silent film successes, including a film called *Peacock Alley* with Mae Murray, which the studio remade as a sound film in 1929. Miss Murray, who was Tiffany's biggest boxoffice attraction of the late 1920's also appeared in such Tiffany features as *The French Doll, Fascination, Broadway Rose, Jazzmania, Circe, Mademoiselle Midnight* and *Fashion row.*

Continuing its penchant for the "society film", the studio moved confidently into the latter days of the silent film era with such offerings as *Souls For Sables, Morals For Men, Borrowed Finery, Pleasures of The Rich* and *Out Of The Storm.* Moreover, the company assured exhibitors it would produce such future offerings as *That Model From Paris, Fools Of Fashion, The Tempest, One Hour Of Love* and *Husband Hunters.* Clearly, Tiffany's goal at that time was to provide theatres with the type of film which later was the staple items of radio!

Only a handful of Tiffany's voiceless features were aimed at the action film audiences, among such films being *Lightning, Snowbound, Raging Seas,* and *The Squared Ring.* Nowhere among Tiffany's early offerings were western features, which is surprising, since such films were easily marketed and cheaply produced.

As the 1920's moved toward their faltering close, however, sound pictures came on the scene and with that, the studio began altering its film production tenets to include westerns and other "B" pictures.

By the arrival of the 1930's, the firm was offering theatres "sound" westerns which starred Ken Maynard, Bob Steele and Rex Lease, the latter alternating in films other than of a western nature. Tiffany introduced its western series in the early summer of 1930 with a film called *Border Romance* which starred Don Terry and Armida. The film was not truly a western in the classic sense, but

In 1931, the Talisman Lot was known as the Tiffany-Stahl Studios, deriving the second portion of its name from that of producer John Stahl, then in charge of Tiffany Production. [Photo courtesy of First Federal Savings, Hollywood/Bruce Torrence, Historical Collection]

the ice had been broken at Tiffany's — to coin a bad expression. At any rate, in June of 1930, the company offered Bob Steele in *Near The Rainbow's End* which was followed that autumn by *Oklahoma Cyclone,* again starring Bob Steele. Then later in October of 1930, with Rex Lease in *Utah Kid.*

Late that year, the firm acquired the services of Ken Maynard, whose contract at Universal had ended in a dispute relating to a western originally titled *Doomed To Die.* After that picture, Maynard left Universal and moved to the Poverty Row studios, and to Tiffany specifically, with the feature *Fighting Through* which Tiffany released late in 1930. Through the next two years, the studio offered a large number of westerns — about twenty in all — some ten of which starred Maynard, and eight of them with Bob Steele. The balance were primarily features which offered

filmgoers the chance to see Rex Lease as a western star, as in *Utah Kid,* released also in October 1930.

Tiffany made a total of seventy sound features, some twenty of which were classified as westerns. Most of the remaining films were what now would be regarded as "soap operas," with a smattering of action melodramas, such as *Drums Of Jeopardy* with June Collyer, Lloyd Hughes and Warner Oland; also *Lost Zeppelin,* a 1929 release which starred Conway Tearle, Richard Cortez and Virginia Valli.

The company's history includes some surprises in feature releases which today are viewed by film officionados with something approaching respect, if only for the surprising casts each had, among them the 1929 feature *Lucky Boy* which starred George Jessel, and *Mamba,* an all-Technicolor feature of 1930 (em-

A scene from **Woman to Woman,** *a Tiffany feature of 1929. Betty Compson is the Ingenue. [Photo from author's collection]*

ploying the old two-strip Technicolor process) which starred Jean Hersholt, Ralph Forbes and Eleanor Boardman.

In the summer of 1930, the firm produced *The Medicine Man* starring Jack Benny and which followed the Tiffany offering of *Molly And Me* which starred Joe E. Brown. *Painted Faces,* a Tiffany release of 1929, was also offered to theatres in two different sound versions — one providing sound-on-disc and one sound-on-film.

By late 1932, however, the nation's economic plight had deepened. Moreover, the sheer novelty of "pictures that talked" had worn off. All around Hollywood small production outfits were closing their doors, unable to wait out the economic crisis. A skeleton production staff remained at the Tiffany studio, turning out endless "Chimp Comedies," a group of short subjects which proved acceptable to film audiences, while at the same time, in-expensive to produce. In such short films as *"Apeing Hollywood"*, chimps, dressed as people, were photographed against undersized sets. Human voices "dubbed in" while the chimps were given bubble gum to chew, in order to obtain "lip movement".

As the "chimp comedies" were keeping a small crew at work at the Tiffany lot, the firm fought to continue in operation.

"We were hoping all the while that the firm would reorganize and get back into production," said sound engineer, John Stransky, not long ago. "When that little miracle didn't occur, well, we just drifted away. At that point, Tiffany became just a part of film history."

Tiffany's story is only one clear-cut section of past film history. Its tale is one that is so often re-told in Hollywood — particularly along Poverty Row that it is seldom recounted.

Tiffany Pictures had two western stars, Ken Maynard and Bob Steele, under contract, both turning out numerous films. Nonetheless, the studio allowed their featured player Rex Lease to make this western, **The Utah Kid** [1930]. Ordinarily, however, Lease appeared in non-western roles at Tiffany. [Photo courtesy of Jan Barfoed]

In its brief history, the Tiffany firm released numerous ''talkie'' westerns, like this one, an early 1932 film. Most of the Tiffany westerns starred either Ken Maynard [10 films] or Bob Steele [8 films]. [Photo courtesy of Richard Bann]

TIFFANY PRODUCTIONS
presents

KEN Maynard

in

"TEXAS GUN-FIGHTER

with his
FAMOUS HORSE
"TARZAN"

DIRECTED BY
PHIL ROSEN
RECORDED BY
RCA PHOTOPHONE
OWNED AND PRODUCE
QUADRUPLE PICTU
INC. LTD.

After a period of retirement, veteran actor Conway Tearle resumed screen activities in the Tiffany feature **The Lost Zeppelin** [1929]. Advertised as "an all dialog" feature which meant that the picture was a "100% talkie," several critics expressed the opinion that Tiffany had subjugated sound to action, since there was so much talking and so little happening in the film.

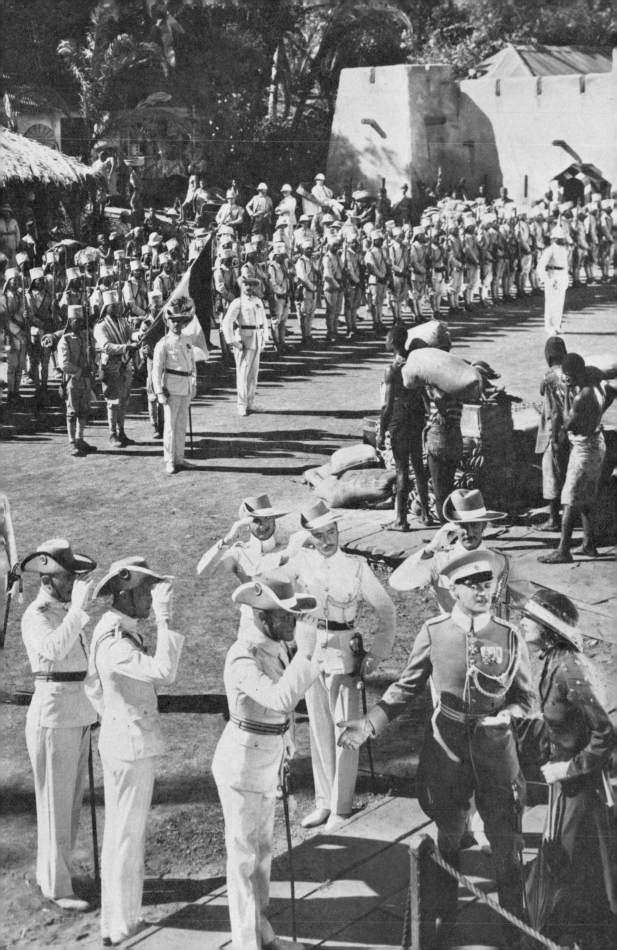

The primitive, early "two-strip" Technicolor was utilized by Tiffany in turning out the 1930 picture **Mamba**, *in which Ralph Forbes, Eleanor Boardman and Jean Hersholt were featured. As may be gleaned from this scene, the company invested rather heavily in the picture, which was directed by Al Rogell.*

Preston Foster in a scene from **THE LAS
MILE,** *which was made by World Wide
a studio that had peripheral connection
with Tiffany.*

Whatever Happened to Grand National?

By the 1930s, the world market for Hollywood films was a large and constantly growing one. Eight major studios in Hollywood were operating at that time. Jointly, these studios turned out nearly 400 features annually; more than 700 short subjects (not counting 500 newsreels) and four serials in the 1935-45 season alone! The independent studios of the era accounted for nearly the same quantity themselves.

Into this burgeoning market stepped Edward R. Alperson, an ambitious thirty-nine year old with a background as a film salesman and a film exchange manager. In the spring of 1936, he helped organize a new film outfit, Grand National Films, Incorporated.

The firm was strengthened, it is said, because James Cagney had quarrelled with the Warner Brothers Studio — to whom he was under contract. Alperson and Cagney came together at that propitious moment, and Grand National Pictures was the result.

The Firm established its New York headquarters at 1270 Sixth Avenue* and a Hollywood office which occupied the Tom Mix residence during a period when the cowboy star was travelling.

Into the ornate home-turned-office building came Alperson with his entourage, which included Carl M. Lesserman, vice-president of the firm, W. C. Bright, who was the company's secretary-treasurer, and Edward Finney, advertising chief of Grand National.

The new organization lost no time in establishing a corporate image, and in adopting an impressive logo consisting of a futuristic clock tower. "The clock tower trade mark we used was the brilliant idea of Eddie Alperson, who reasoned that we could then advertise 'It's always time for a Grand National release,' or such variations as 'it's time to see a Grand National film'; or 'the timeless features'," Edward Finney stated to this author.

As the firm worked at the details of organization, it acquired the studios which formerly had housed Educational Films, the firm which had already produced a long string of short subjects which were released principally through Fox, but which had moved its production activities to the East. When Alperson and his cohorts finished refurbishing the Hollywood lot, they moved their offices to that address, giving the appearance of having come to Hollywood to stay.

*Using First Division Picture Exchanges as its distribution nucleus.

This lot began life as the home of Educational Pictures. Here it is shown as it appeared in 1937, when it housed Edward Alperson's Grand National Pictures. Following the bankruptcy of the Grand National firm, the lot briefly was in possession of producer Franklyn Warner, eventually however, becoming the PRC Studio. [Photo courtesy of First Federal Savings, Hollywood, Bruce Torrence — Historical Collection.]

Eventually, Alperson was able to establish an impressive list of producers whom he believed capable of providing the corporation with an adequate number of releases. B. F. Zeidman, George Hirliman, Max and Arthur Alexander, Zion Myers, and a sizable additional group of producers eventually flocked to the Alperson setup to join the firm which had landed the services of James Cagney!

The depression year of 1936 was Grand National's initial one as a full-scale production-distribution organization. That Fall, the company impressed the trade with their release of a feature titled, *In His Steps* based on a novel first published in 1899, and which had rolled up an impressive sale of more than eight million copies. It was a good choice for Grand National to offer among the firm's initial releases. As a film, it was as well made as many major releases of the time. Moreover, the film version starred Eric Linden, then a popular player.

Originally, the feature was offered under the title *Sins of The Children*. It was eventually released under the same title as the novel from which it was adopted, however.

Close on the heels of that release, Grand National offered its first western, a feature titled, *Devil On Horseback* which producer George Hirliman made in a color process which the producer called "Hirlicolor", but which in reality was Cinecolor.

This full-color feature was joined in Grand National's releases of 1936 by such offerings as a John Payne musical titled, *Hats Off* and such action-melodramas as *White Legion*, *Yellow Cargo* and *Captain Calamity*.

These 1936 offerings were somewhat reminiscent of those which had earlier been released through Grand National Distributing Corporation which in 1935 and into early 1936, had been offering such films as *Dance Band* with Buddy Rogers, and *Bridge of Sighs* with Onslow Stevens. These films were not made by Grand National, but helped the firm to get its film distribution network into operation.

Edward Finney, in charge of advertising and publicity for Grand National, was in the meantime preparing to try his wings as a film producer, wisely reasoning that a new western star would bring Grand National a great deal of attention. With that idea in mind, he had cast about for a personable young man whom Finney could build into Hollywood stardom.

Finney ultimately learned of a cowboy singer who was currently starring as *Cowboy Tom* on a WSM radio series. The young man had never made a film, but he projected a likable enough image on radio. His name was Tex Ritter.

"First, of course, I had to convince other Grand National officials that I'd made the proper choice in this case. To do that, I knew that we must prepare a brief screen test. So I sent for Tex," states Finney.

"I knew a top flight makeup man at Paramount — a fellow named Eddie Senz," continued Finney. "We hastily made up a screen test at the Paramount lot, on a sort of western-style saloon set they had there. Well, Tex sang a song, read some dialog, and generally looked the handsome, virile cowboy I was looking for. That test impressed Alperson and the others at Grand

44

Producer-director Edward Finney, as he appeared during one of the years that he was with Grand National. [Photo from author's collection]

National, and we were on our way.

"The first film Tex and I made for Alperson's firm was a feature called *Song of the Gringo*, which provided a competent cast alongside Ritter — 'Fuzzy' Knight, Monte Blue, Bud Osborne and others.

"We shot that film at the Talisman Studios — the interior scenes that is — and the exteriors out at Monogram Ranch, in Newhall, California."

Before a year was past, Tex Ritter had captured the public's attention, and in fact, had established himself in sixth place in the favorites among western stars, a fact which was a source of honor both for producer Edward Finney and for Grand National.

In fact, theatre owners everywhere were suddenly finding the new studio's releases exceedingly commendable.

Mr. Boggs Steps Out which starred Stuart Erwin; *Bank Alarm* with Conrad Nagel, and James Newill in *Renfrew of the Royal Mounted,* all gave assurance that Grand National's pictures would please filmgoers everywhere.

This optimistic viewpoint was simply strengthened by the release of James Cagney's first Grand National film, an exciting feature called *Great Guy* (1936) which dealt with the subject of smashing the weights and measures rackets, and which was based upon a series of Cosmopolitan magazine stories of the time. The film was on a par with the fast-moving pictures in which Cagney had starred at Warner Brothers, and promised even greater Cagney offerings under the Grand National label in the future.

"We didn't know it at the time, but Alperson was about to make a tragic decision where Jimmy Cagney's next

45

Grand National inaugurated the popular **Renfrew of the Royal Mounted** series with James Newill and Carol Hughes appearing in a feature titled simply **Renfrew of the Royal Mounted**, which was released in 1937. [Photo courtesy of Jan Barfoed]

Tex Ritter's first screen appearance was in a Grand National western, **Song of the Gringo** [1936]. The scene [left] is from **Riders of the Rockies** offered by Grand National in 1937. [Photo courtesy of Jan Barfoed]

Here is budding screen star Rita Hayworth appearing in the film, **Trouble in Texas** made by Mohawk Film Corporation, but released through Grand National. At left is Yakima Canutt, later to become a well-known stunt director. The leading man, at right, is Tex Ritter. [Photo courtesy of Jan Barfoed]

film was concerned," says Edward Finney, recalling the next events at Grand National.

"Alperson had the foresight to buy a story called *Angels With Dirty Faces,* which he intended to turn into a film in which Cagney was to star for Grand National," Finney continued.

"Instead, with that story on Alperson's desk, mind you, he allowed himself to be talked into making instead, a musical called, *Something To Sing About.* As it turned out for Cagney and for Grand National, however, it should have been named *Something To Cry About,* for that film bankrupted the corporation — eventually wiped it out completely.

"Several of us had tried to reason with Alperson. 'Look', we argued, 'do *Angels With Dirty Faces* first. After all, you've tied up $25,000 for the rights to that story, which is a perfect one for Cagney's talents.' "

Finney and his supporters lost their argument however. Alperson went ahead, permitting director Victor Schertzinger — who'd written the screenplay for *Something To Sing About* — to make that film, which ended up costing about $900,000 — far more than the original budget it had been allotted and much more than the studio was able to finance at that time.

Public reception to the feature *Something To Sing About* was instant apathy. Reviews of the film were not helpful, either. Within a matter of days after the picture's release in 1937 it was obvious that the film could not recoup its costs. Grand National was ruined.

The company continued to release features through 1939, including some fine "B" films such as *Wallaby Jim Of The Islands* which starred George Houston, and the imported film *Juggernaut* in which Boris Karloff was starred. But even these films and for a time the profitable Tex Ritter westerns, were unable to save the studio from a slow financial death.

The next year was an anti-climactic one, neither as busy nor as impressive a period as 1937 had been. There were only about a dozen features put into copyright by Grand National during 1938, among them one of the popular "Shadow" pictures (*International Crime*) and a handful of westerns, including *Whirlwind Horseman* with Ken Maynard. For the most part, however, the schedule was unimpressive. The firm clearly was in trouble.

If its production schedule hadn't made its financial troubles evident the year before, Grand National did so in the early months of 1939, for its new schedule of films for that year was extremely thin and unimpressive. Most of the few pictures it offered were westerns of extremely cheap production value, including *Ride 'Em Cowgirl* and *Singing Cowgirl* with newcomer Dorothy Page starring. (Anticipating "Womens Lib" no doubt).

In that year, Grand National ceased to exist, its clock tower tolling the company's own death knell. All told, even if one counts its predecessor's history as a distributing corporation (1935 and early 1936), we total less than four years in the final tally.

By an odd quirk, the name still exists. Its namesake in Great Britain is still very much alive, with offices at 13 Dean Street, London.

Somehow, the survival of the name

By 1939 it was apparent that Grand National was in financial trouble Most of "name" players and technicians had left the studio, causing it to attempt to develop new stars, such as "the world's only singing cowgirl," Dorothy Page, shown here in a scene from the 1939 western, **Ride 'Em Cowgirl**. Milton Frome is shown here with Miss Page. Although Grand National offered exhibitors a handful of Miss Page's films, she generated no enthusiasm among western fans, and soon retired from the screen. [Photo courtesy of Jan Barfoed]

makes the Grand National story much less final and much more intriguing. Another reason why the name of the releasing organization has remained so familiar with film collectors has been the number of 16mm prints of Grand National films (about 70 pictures counting those offered by Grand National Distributors) which have been made since the 35mm prints were originally made. Post Pictures of New York, and other 16mm distributors, have issued copies of various Grand National releases, and so helped to keep the firm's history, and its name, before film enthusiasts.

With so much of the Grand National output available for re-examination, it would seem that we could make a fair appraisal of its contributions to Hollywood history. Unfortunately, like PRC which followed them, Grand National is difficult to assess. For one thing, its films were the product of many individual organizations, and production outfits such as Condor and Coronado Films, though the firm also produced part of its feature offerings, it's true.

As a whole, Grand National's films were not exceedingly bad, though many lacked the element of real action so essential to most pictures that are successful in the "B" run districts. Even such Grand National pictures as *International Crime* and *Hideout In The Alps* which, by their very titles promise a high degree of action, end up as very ordinary and lethargic talkies.

The action scene of Grand National lacked the punch, which studios like Republic put a great deal of money into creating. There was clearly too much "sound-stage" shooting in its overall output and not enough location work.

Grand National's pictures suffer if compared with Mascot's product (1929-35), for instance. With the "star power" of the Grand National roster, the firm far outstripped Mascot. Yet, in the final analysis, Alperson's group of producers seemed unable to catch the flavor of the tastes wielded by patrons of sidestreet theatres. The result was that much of the company's product seemed to be made to fit both theatres frequented by "action fans" and those more likely to play prestige and musical films! Even Cagney's pictures for Grand National were "toned down".

Now, every one of Hollywood's well-established "Poverty Row" outfits has turned out a crop of prestige films, it is true. Grand National cannot be blamed for that. After all Republic made the Tito Quizar and Vera Ralston musicals. And Monogram had its share of films like Belita in *Lady, Let's Dance*. It's all right to make a few prestige films, but not if one tries to make obviously Class "B" features fit into the prestige houses of the world. That, if anything, was Grand National's major sin.

Considering the period in which the Grand National firm was operating, and the company's intended market, its films are virtually all acceptable entries. Had the firm continued, it is quite possible that they might have given Republic and Monogram quite stiff competition, and PRC too.

The final days of Grand National were both eventful and discouraging. The death of the firm was preceded on February 25, 1939, by the resignation of Edward R. Alperson. In less than a year, trade journals disclosed the facts that Grand National had some $700,000 indebtedness outstanding.

Earlier, however, in the February 5, 1938, issue of the trade journal, *Box*

The first of two Grand National features in which James Cagney appeared, **Great Guy** [1937] was an action feature quite like Cagney's most successful hits made at Warner Brothers. In this particular feature, Cagney played the role of a pull-no-punches government man, out to smash the weights and measures racket. [Photo courtesy of Academy of Motion Picture Arts and Sciences]

Here's an informal view of some of the principals who figured in the Grand National feature, **Great Guy** [1937]. The director is John Blystone; the cameraman, Jack MacKenzie, and of course, the star, James Cagney. This feature was made at the RKO-Pathe Studios in Culver City, some time prior to Grand National's acquisition of its own studio setup, the former Educational Studios. [Photo courtesy of Erwin Dumbrille]

In the final tragic days of Grand National's history, and after Edward L. Alperson had ceased to be head of the firm, producer Franklyn Warner [center] undertook a feature titled, **Isle of Destiny** to be released through a revitalized Grand National, as headed by E. W. Hammons. When Hammons failed to get the loans he counted on, the firm finally, ignominiously perished. Warner then released **Isle of Destiny** through RKO. Other principals in the above photo are Arthur Hoerl [left] who wrote the screenplay, and Samuel Berkowitz [standing] executive manager of Franklyn Warner's production unit, Fine Art Pictures. Star of the picture, William Gargan is seated at right. [Photo courtesy of Academy of Motion Picture Arts and Sciences]

Office, short subject producer E. W. Hammons indicated that since his contract with 20th Century-Fox was due to expire, he was slightly interested in entering into the Grand National problem. He further suggested that he wanted $1,000,000 "on the line" before he did so. (His demand was odd, in view of his firm's own indebtedness at the time!)

While all this was transpiring, the Grand National lot was idle, its reported overhead running $35,000 per week! Since an auction at the lot failed to raise much — furniture and other assets raising but $7,800 — it was clear that something would have to be done soon, if the Grand National label were to be reactivated.

Soon afterward, a flurry of trade announcements indicated that Hammons was seeking financial aid for the firm from the U. S. Government's Reconstruction Finance Corporation, the hopes for which were stifled by a later announcement, in early 1940, that the RFC loan was refused. Subsequently, a bankruptcy referee was named in the case. Remaining assets of Grand National at that point included some twenty-six feature pictures and about 500 Educational (E. W. Hammons) short subjects. The studio which bore the Grand National name, originally built by Hammons, had mortgages against the facility which were immense — Electrical Research Products, Incorporated, for example, entering a $245,000 mortgage suit against the "Educational Studio".

When this tangle of unpaid bills began to be thrown at the Grand National Firm, it became clear that no amount of reorganization would save the company. The Grand National phase of the Poverty Row story was all too clearly over. In its brief history, the corporation had lighted up the skies of Hollywood with a faint star, an ambitious promise. Its chapter of Poverty Row's story ending on a tragic note — like so many others along the mythical street.

In This Corner:
A Monogram

IN October of 1929, the U. S. stock market took a gigantic plunge, signalling firmly the outset of a nation-wide economic paralysis. The condition was destined to remain virtually until the beginnings of World War II. It was an unlikely time in which to establish a motion picture studio; nonetheless, dozens of firms were established after 1929, among which was Monogram Pictures. At first, Monogram saw its films distributed to small theatres where standard admissions were ten cents and twenty cents, but as admissions ascended so did Monogram's income.

Founded by W. Ray Johnston, a precocious young man from Bristow, Iowa, the Monogram effort was not the young man's first film organization. By the time he was twenty-three, Johnston had graduated from school, and from early work experience as the treasurer for a small motion picture outfit known as Syndicate Pictures*, the job led to a responsible position with the old Thanhouser Studio, at its operation in Florida.

With the coming of 1924, Johnston struck out on his own, establishing a firm which boldly called itself Big Productions Corporation, which incidentally was responsible for some of the important silent chapter plays of that era, as was Johnston's later firm, Rayart.

The coming of "talkies", however, led Johnston to establish a new firm, the one he christened Monogram Pictures. From its beginnings, Monogram dealt through a group of distribution franchise holders — 20 of them by 1933 which blanketed 39 geographical areas in North America. This arrangement gave Monogram a group of distributors which required little real investment in the exchanges by the parent firm.

From its inception until early in 1935, the firm went about the task of assembling distributors, and at the same time a stable of producers whom Johnston felt were capable of supplying Monogram with diverse and profitable productions. These were made at rental sound stages in all parts of Hollywood — for Johnston's organization at first had no studio facilities of its own.*

Details of picture production were placed under the guidance of Trem Carr, who had earlier joined the

---

*Johnston later usurped the name for a short-lived firm which he and Trem Carr operated before the Monogram firm began, and indeed for short time after Monogram got into operation.

*The original Monogram studios were at the Talisman lot, at 4516 Sunset Boulevard in Hollywood. For a time, the firm operated a studio here, later at 1040 North Las Palmas, which was the company's address in 1934, when it merged with Republic. When it resumed operation, in 1936, Monogram simply occupied space at the Universal lot, then moved to its own facilities at Sunset Drive and Hoover — its final home.

This is the final home of the old
Monogram Pictures, which now is a
TV Station. During the period that
Monogram occupied this setup, the
firm was busily releasing such series
as **Charlie Chan, The Bowery Boys,
Snuffy Smith,** and many more.
[*Photo courtesy of Erwin Dumbrille*]

The widow of actor Wallace Reid produced **Paradise Isle** [1937] for Monogram which Arthur G. Collins directed. [Mrs. Reid was story editor for Monogram at the time.] The picture featured actress Movita, who'd achieved some fame in M-G-M's **Mutiny on the Bounty**. Monogram's publicity claimed the picture had been filmed in Samoa; however, it's unlikely their camera crews journeyed any farther than Catalina, or a similar "off shore" spot not far distant from the California coast in making this feature.

Johnston circle. Carr's leadership of Monogram's production side, in fact, gave him an important voice in the overall firm. Under his operation, followed such producers as M. H. Hoffman, I. E. Chadwick, Paul Malvern, and so on.

Beginning in 1931, Monogram undertook actual release of features, its early westerns including Tom Tyler in *Galloping Thru*. Production was somewhat limited until the next year, however.

In that season, 1932, the company released an impressive total of 32 pictures, including Ginger Rogers in *The Thirteenth Guest* (a feature which Monogram re-made a few years afterward with Helen Parrish), *Strange Adventure, Klondike, Man From Arizona, Broadway To Cheyenne, Hidden Valley,* and *Girl From Calgary*.

In 1933, Monogram presented exhibitors with about two dozen more features, including a screen version of Anna Sewell's children's novel *Black Beauty*. At this time, the firm's western fare was made up almost entirely of offerings which starred either Bob Steele or Rex Bell. (Steele's father Robert N. Bradbury was a director and a script writer at Monogram during this time).

Later in that same year, John Wayne was added to the list of Monogram players, his initial film for the studio *Sagebrush Trail* being released in December of that year. The film was made for Monogram by Paul Malvern

A close associate of friend W. Ray Johnston was Monogram's Vice President for Production, Scott R. Dunlap shown here in the mid-1930s. [Photo from author's collection]

He founded a great many film companies, and was associated with even more firms in the cinema circle, but it is with Monogram Pictures that the name W. Ray Johnston is associated now. [Photo from author's collection]

and his producing organization, Lone Star Productions, and was the first of several such films in which Wayne appeared for Monogram.

That same year, the firm captured a surprising honor from the editors of *Parent's Magazine* for the Monogram film version of *Oliver Twist*, which starred Dickie Moore, Irving Pichel and Jackie Searle. The feature, produced by Herbert Brennon and I. E. Chadwick, was a quite faithful adaptation of Charles Dickens' classic novel. The magazine award spotlighted the firm and its production activities of that time, making the rest of Hollywood, for the first time, aware of the new studio and its capabilities.

Throughout 1934 and early in 1935, Monogram continued its ambitious program of feature releases, totalling some three dozen films in 1934 alone.

In 1935, the Monogram label was suspended, the company and its assets absorbed in a merger with the new Republic firm, a company spearheaded by Herbert J. Yates of Consolidated Film Laboratories.

Before the merger was completed that year, Monogram marketed a few offerings under its own label, including a feature called *Mysterious Mr. Wong,* which starred Bela Lugosi. (That feature became the basis later of a brief series which offered Boris Karloff in the role which Lugosi assayed in this initial feature.) *Make A Million* (with Charles Starrett in one of his rare non-western roles), *Sing Sing Nights,* which featured Conway Tearle, were three among the releases that comprised the entire Monogram output of that year.

A few pictures, including John Wayne in *Paradise Canyon* and *Rainbow Valley* were made by Monogram's facility but were released through the Republic organization. In 1936, the Monogram firm did not operate. Indeed, Johnston and Trem Carr were corporate officials

The jailbird in the picture is Eric Linden and the doting, worried female is the talented Jean Arthur starring in one of her earlier films.

Both Monogram and Republic Pictures saw fit to expend countless World War II dollars on production of iceskating "extravaganzas" such as this one, in which Monogram starred its contract player Belita, who was a not-too loud answer to Republic's Vera Hruba Ralston, who in turn, was an attempt to "cash in" on the current craze for Sonja Henie films. [Photo from author's collection]

at the new Republic lot. As far as the motion picture world knew then, Monogram was a thing of the past, a memory to add to the dozens of others which made Hollywood's past.

In 1937, personalities within the Republic operation began to clash.* "Let's put it this way," Nat Levine, then an official of the Republic firm, explained to this author, "there was some dissatisfaction at certain figures who had joined Republic from the original Monogram operation."

Whatever the underlying cause of the rift, Johnston and Trem Carr made their final bows at Republic, and left there to revive the Monogram label. In 1937, they resumed operations and released about 20 feature films. This number included such pictures as the westerns *Where Trails Divide, Stars Over Arizona* and *Riders of the Dawn,* and such

*One generally circulated story is that Trem Carr of Monogram was almost continually "at sword's point" with Republic's chief stockholder, Herbert Yates.

features as *Hoosier Schoolboy* with Mickey Rooney and Anne Nagel, and a well-made feature which was made from Bret Harte's famous short story *The Luck of Roaring Camp.*

At the time, Monogram operated out of rental space at Universal, having no studio of its own. Johnston and Carr cast about for a studio they could obtain at a sales price that was suitable to the economic slump. Eventually, they found such a layout, of course, for film studio space was little in demand prior to World War II.

The coming of the 1938-1939 season caused officials at Monogram to pause for an advertising review of their past triumphs. In a sprawling advertising brochure, they recounted a few of the boxoffice successes they had already fostered, including Jackie Cooper in *Boy of the Streets,* Jean Parker and Eric Linden in *Romance of the Limberlost,*

*Mickey Rooney broke into motion pictures as Mickey "Himself" McGuire. From that series of comedies, he made his way into juvenile roles in pictures made by Mascot and Monogram, among others. This is a production still from the Monogram feature **The Healer** [1935] in which Mickey Rooney was co-featured with Judith Allen. Although a Monogram feature, it was released by Republic during the brief period that Monogram was merged with the Republic organization.*
This was one of Monogram's "kid star" films, others included pictures with Jackie Cooper, Jackie Moran, Martin Spellman, Frankie Darro, the "Bowery Boys," Marcia Mae Jones and June Preisser.

Proof that Monogram Pictures attempted to scale the heights created by Universal's "musicals," this 1943 feature provides you a look at Monogram features of a class A lineage, if not of that budget category. [Photo from the author's collection]

Mickey Rooney in *Hoosier Schoolboy*, Movita and John Carroll in *Rose of the Rio Grande*, Evelyn Venable in *My Old Kentucky Home* and Movita and Warren Hull in *Paradise Isle*, of which more will be said later. Such features as *Atlantic Flight* a relatively low budget Monogram offering, rated a collective bow from the many theatres who relied on Monogram products to give them impetus over the big "first run" theatres of their area.

The western pictures which issued from Monogram in the early 1930's impressed film reviewers of various trade journals and other periodicals of that time. Jack Randall in *Stars Over Arizona* and *Riders of the Dawn*, Tom Keene in *Where Trails Divide* and Tim McCoy in *West of Rainbow's End* and *Code of the Rangers* all gave notice prior to 1938 that Monogram was one of the best outfits on Poverty Row.

"In 1938 and 1939, it is our intention," wrote Monogram President W. Ray Johnston, "to release a schedule of 26 features and 16 westerns composed of those boxoffice elements that the theatres of our country are demanding." Just what those theatres were demanding was anything which would keep the ticket offices busy, of course. In line with a belief that their little firm could produce such boxoffice magic, Monogram announced two features starring Jackie Cooper, *Streets of New York* and *That Old Gang of Mine,* and a trio of films which were designed for actress Movita and co-star John Carroll, *Lost Legion, Isle of Terror* and *Under Northern Lights.*

This was the period in which the studio revived the "Mr. Wong Detective" series. In its new form, the series offered Boris Karloff in the starring role. Four new features of the series were announced, *Mr. Wong In Chinatown, Mystery of Mr. Wong, Mr. Wong — Detective,* and *Mr. Wong at Headquarters.* The series, immensely popular with readers of *Collier's* magazine, practically guaranteed the success of the film offerings, which had the added boxoffice appeal of Boris Karloff, who by then was a filmgoer's favorite. Karloff was a graduate of Universal's "Frankenstein" company of players, among other stepping stones to fame.

For the 1937-38 season, Monogram advertised western offerings which included eight films starring Jack Randall, another eight which featured Tex Ritter. The two series — the *Lone Star* offerings in which Jack Randall was featured and the *Gold Rush* series which producer Edward Finney churned out with his "star find" Tex Ritter — did not seem as impressive as some of the earlier ones which offered John Wayne, Tim McCoy and that ilk. But they were highly saleable to lovers of films which were built about the sagebrush territory.

Like virtually all film studios of the 1930's and earlier, Monogram invested relatively little in the production of western pictures, such films being regarded by film makers as "bread and butter" offerings, inevitably almost identical in production values and stories, and worthy only of enough attention to assure acceptability, but never to rise above others in their category. It is a narrow viewpoint, altered by the time of the early 1940's when the films of Gene Autry, John Wayne, Roy Rogers and a few others had shown just how much power at the boxoffice good western stars and films could offer.

There is a curious dichotomy to this tendency of Hollywood production

63

Julie [Kathleen Burke] plans to send Norah [Maureen O'Conner] away to school, as Chuck [Jackie Cooper] objects in front of Mrs. Brennan [Majorie Main] and Ronoke [Robert Emmett O'Conner]. Gordon Elliott smiles encouragingly. The feature is a 1938 release turned out before Elliott came to added screen fame as "Wild Bill" Elliott.

The screen figure of Earl Derr Bigger's fictional detective had made untold profits for Fox film, and its successor, 20th Century Fox. Here, during World War II years, the series became one of the properties of "Poverty Row", and more particularly, of Monogram Pictures. [Photo from the author's collection]

When 20th Century-Fox dropped the Charlie Chan films, Monogram picked up the rights to the series, and proceeded to feature Sydney Toler as the famed oriental detective, just as Fox had done for a time. This series of films, [in both the Fox and Monogram versions] is still shown on TV. The scene is from **Dangerous Money**, 1946, Monogram.

Producer Sam Katzman just didn't know what money-makers he possessed in the winning combination of Leo Gorcey and Huntz Hall. Nonetheless, Katzman produced several "East Side Kids" features which were offered through Monogram prior to the long period that the kids went under contract to producer, Jan Grippo, who also released his features through Monogram. [Photos from author's collection]

firms to ignore the western. Because most of the world regards motion pictures as an art form — which certainly they are — it tends to overlook the financial aspects of cinema. Not only dollars taken in by a given film, but dollars SPENT in making that picture are significant. Sometimes a single feature production would gross thousands of dollars in a single day of showings in theatres across the nation, whereas the studio which produced it might, after payment of all operating expenses, gross not much more than one hundred thousand dollars for an entire year! Monogram for example, claimed that boxoffice grosses for their early 1930 film *Boy of the Streets* occasionally went as high as fourteen thousand dollars in a single ''booking'' but in 1937, Monogram grossed only $60,279 from its entire operation!

Perhaps a false economy within the Monogram organization prevented the firm from ever making much of an impression in the western genre, for example. Whatever the underlying reason, Monogram's westerns never were as impressive as those made over at Republic. For one thing, the ''stock music'' inherent in Monogram's sagebrush epics militated against their serious consideration. Nonetheless, reviewers of the 1930's and 1940's tended to view Monogram's westerns with a sort of paternal pat on the back.

Considering the purpose of Monogram's pictures and the audiences for

In 1933, Monogram released this western **Crashing Broadway** *which featured Rex Bell. [Photo courtesy of Jan Barfoed]*

which they were designed, the studio's general output was NOT really deficient. At their best, theirs could be quite pleasant little films of a low-budget type, as witness John Carroll and Movita in *Wolf Call* (1939) and Warren Hull in *Paradise Isle* (1937), Eddie Albert in the fascinating and well-paced drama *Strange Voyage*, or Frankie Darro and Manton Moreland in *Irish Luck* (1939). The "Bowery Boys" series, too, is amusing, as television has made us again and again aware.

Monogram's Buck Jones films were quite satisfying, and *West of Rainbow's End* with Tim McCoy is as good a "modern western" as you'll find. David Sharpe in *Silver Stallion* is a pleasing western, too. Producer Edward Finney may be proud of that modest little picture, as well as the Tex Ritter westerns he made for Monogram release.

To discuss the history of Monogram without mentioning some of that firm's "unusual" feature offerings would be a gross omission indeed. For example, a modest feature called *The Adventures of Chico* was a Monogram offering which, while not a sensational feature, nonetheless was an entertaining one, a sort of forerunner of the Disney features and documentary short subjects. Reputedly filmed in Mexico, the film was the simple story of a Mexican boy and a "road-runner." That Monogram feature later was cut into a short subject which was released on the 16mm width of film as *"Roadrunner Battles Rattlesnake,"* and which was an entry for many years in the Castle Films catalog, even after United World Films (Universal) acquired the Castle firm and their films.

Eddie Albert played in a Monogram feature titled *Strange Voyage* (a film in which Elena Verdugo also appeared).

Reminiscent of Warner's expensive feature *Treasure of Sierra Madre,* which starred Humphrey Bogart, Tim Holt and Walter Huston, the Monogram film captured much of the suspense, loneliness and the unfulfilled quest which the more expensive Bogart film expressed.

Of more than passing interest, too, was the Monogram feature *Thirty Fathoms Below* which starred Arthur Lake and Lon Chaney, Jr. The primary setting of this color film was Tarpon Springs, Florida, and the actual "blessing of the sponge fishing fleet" by the Greek Orthodox Church of the Tarpon Springs Community. Although the fictional tale which involves a gangster who "hides out" in Tarpon Springs, joins the sponge fishermen and finds moral regeneration, is trite, the picture emerges as a sort of semi-documentary worth viewing. Moreover, it is a worthwhile release of the Monogram features, which covered in all, about 25 years of time.

In reviewing Monogram's history of film production, it is well to give a more than cursory glance to the many films which the studio made which were based — however loosely — upon novels or short stories, such as *Oliver Twist* and *Black Beauty*, which already were mentioned. *Luck of Roaring Camp*, also touched upon, and *Jane Eyre,* which was based upon Charlotte Bronte's famous novel. Also, the Indiana author Edward Eggleston was well represented by the Monogram feature *Hoosier Schoolmaster* in which Douglas Montgomery and Charlotte Henry starred.

In 1939, Samuel Goldwyn made a rather artificial film version of the Broadway play *Dead End* in which Goldwyn starred Humphrey Bogart with

69

Huntz Hall, Leo Gorcey and certain other juveniles who were brought to Hollywood from the stage version. Universal Pictures saw great financial possibilities in these juveniles, and took over the services of the youths after Goldwyn had finished with them, proceeding to turn out a number of feature pictures.

Eventually, a producer at Monogram, Sam Katzman, acquired the screen services of some of the young people who had earlier appeared in the Goldwyn film, and re-christening the "gang" as "The East Side Kids" made several features for Monogram, including *East Side Kids* and *Mr. Muggs Steps Out.*

Monogram offered theatre managers a modest but delightful screen version of Charles Dickens' classic **Oliver Twist.** The Herbert Brennon production featured Dickie Moore, Irving Pichel, William Boyd and Jackie Searle.

However, it was Jan Grippo, another Monogram producer, who saw continuing profits in the "Kids" and their antics. Under Grippo's guidance, then, the team was renamed the "Bowery Boys" and eventually completed about a half of a hundred features both for Monogram and for Allied Artists,* the successors to the

*"We just about owned Monogram," Huntz Hall once said.

Monogram mantle. Under Grippo's productions and guidance, "The Bowery Boys" proved themselves real "mortgage lifters" at Monogram and, later, at Allied Artists. Until the "lads" were well into their adult years they continued to appear in the series, in the last few of which Huntz Hall led the group without the assistance of Leo Gorcey who had unfortunately turned to alcohol by then — some saying because Leo was brokenhearted at the accidental death of his father Bernard Gorcey, who portrayed the character of "Louie" in so many of the Bowery Boys films.

The long-time box office success of both the "East Side Kids" series and later, the "Bowery Boys" tends to obscure the many other series which Monogram successfully carried on for varying lengths of time, among them the *Renfrew of the Mounties* films which series the firm acquired from Grand National, and the *Charlie Chan* films, which the firm made from 1943 to the end of their existence, and which had been inspired by an earlier series which the old Fox Film Corporation and later 20th Century-Fox firm had begun.

Other features at Monogram included a shabbily made series which were inspired by the comic strip character of "Snuffy Smith" and western offerings of the "Range Busters." In fact, Monogram produced more "series films" than any other studio and maintained unusually high quality on some of these series, such as the "Bowery Boys" offering and the "Charlie Chan" films, which were uniformly well done, from beginning to end. Other series, like the "Tailspin Tommy" offerings of Monogram, were very ordinary action films, capable of, at best, filling the lower spot on a double feature program.

The pictures mentioned here helped make Monogram generally a profitable firm, both for the studio and for the countless theatres of the world who looked to it for films which would attract audiences.

By the end of World War II, Monogram (which stood practically on the doorstep of becoming Allied Artists) had cornered the services of quite a few players well known by audiences who attended the smaller neighborhood theatres and those in America's "rural hinterlands." These players, while not usually under exclusive contract to Monogram or its producers, nonetheless were frequent players for that organization. The roster included at various times Leo Gorcey, Huntz Hall, Gabriel Dell, Gale Storm, Johnny Sheffield (he played Bomba in a long string of Monogram features), Belita, John Carroll, Warren Hull, Duncan Renaldo, Sidney Toler and Gilbert Roland.

In November, 1946, Allied Artists Productions, Inc., was established as a subsidiary of Monogram, with S. Steve Broidy as president and Johnston as chairman of the board. In 1953, the Monogram name was dropped, and the firm became Allied Artists Pictures Corporation, with a subsidiary in TV production, of course, for television by then was a serious contender to theatres. But it was as Monogram Pictures that the firm wrote the sizable page in Hollywood's history.

By the 1950's however, the firm had chosen to become Allied Artists, in part because the film market was changing. Through the years the name "Monogram" had come to stand for a type of entertainment geared to the small neighborhood theatre, the rural show house, the subsequent-run theatre. It

In 1933, Monogram won an award from prestigious Parents' Magazine for the delightful film, **Oliver Twist,** in which Dickie Moore [left] and Irving Pichel [right] played the leading roles and in which William Boyd played a prominent part also.

A scant three years old at the time that the company turned out **Oliver Twist,** the Monogram firm quickly discovered from the film that lachrymose movies starring child stars were pure gold at the box-office. Accordingly, in ensuing years, they churned out dozens of such offerings as **Barefoot Boy, Boy of the Streets, Hoosier Schoolboy, Tomboy, Freckles,** and many more.

Bob Steele certainly appeared in numerous films made by many different studios, such as this one, a 1933 Monogram offering. This western was titled, **Galloping Romeo** and the other players shown in this picture are Ernie Adams and Edwin Brady. [Photo courtesy of Jan Barfoed]

was an image the firm wished to abandon.

So with some regret, the established name was quietly laid aside, and was replaced by a very pretentious appearing trademark which proclaimed the firm to be "Allied Artists," a name which was impressive and prim sounding, and which was new, but similar to other Hollywood names of the past — Alliance Films, Allied Pictures Corporation, Allied Producers and Distributors, etc. — which engendered the idea that the company had been around for a bit.

It must be borne in mind that the Monogram firm was always more or less a label for independent producers which grouped together largely for convenience in distribution of their film product, and for the prestige which the Monogram name gave to their productions. It was an approach which the successor firm continued, albeit with much more impressive productions than those which Monogram had undertaken.

By means of the Allied Artists firm, the story of Monogram continues. Like the Republic organization, the skeleton of the original organization still exists, although both operate no actual film studio, of course. But like some stubborn ghosts from an age long gone, they linger.

Many Poverty Row producers used the rental stages of RKO-Pathe, at Culver City, California, shown here as it appeared in about mid-1930. (Photo courtesy Bruce Torrence Collection c/o First Federal of Hollywood.

To The Republic
For Which Yates Stands

IN those halcyon days when all America rode the crest of a wave of prosperity, Hollywood's aging "King of the Custard Pies and Keystone Cops" — Mack Sennett — had invested heavily in a sprawling studio that Sennett, its original owner, foresaw as a shrine to the golden future of screen comedy. Changing audience tastes and a crushing economic depression, however, soon ended Sennett's reign in Hollywood. A bankruptcy court moved in and shuttered his place, as had happened so many times to businesses during that period.

Nat Levine, then operating his Mascot Pictures from a small battery of offices over a contractor's warehouse on Santa Monica Boulevard, was the first to seriously consider buying the Sennett property. He approached Trem Carr and Ray Johnston over at Monogram about going in with Mascot on the purchase. The Monogram chieftains, however, turned a cold shoulder to the idea. The lot and its concomitant expenses of operation would be too much, they felt, even for two film outfits to shoulder, and as a result Monogram preferred to make films on "rental stages" as always.

Undaunted, Levine decided to bear the burden of taking on the "valley lot" as it was already known, armed only with an option to buy the place. As the 1930's moved toward the half-way point, Mascot took over the premises (having deserted the contractor's "spare" offices) and prepared to continue production at its newly acquired sound stages, part of which would rent to Chesterfield Pictures.*

Simultaneously, Herbert J. Yates, founder of Consolidated Film Laboratories, was entering production with an organization called Republic Pictures, which was first based at Universal. Because both Monogram and Mascot were customers of the Consolidated Laboratories, the sheer volume of their business convinced Yates that one large independent film production firm would be a more profitable enterprise than three small ones. This idea in mind, Yates approached Johnston and Levine. Why not weld their two firms with a smaller one, Liberty, and together with Republic, form one large firm? The principals ultimately agreed on the details and the deal was made.

Yates had resurrected the name "Republic" from a World War I era film laboratory he had once organized and with that name, they began organizational planning of Republic Pictures. At first, Johnston was president of the resulting firm, with Levine a producer and vice president for the new organization. Yates had considerable money in the venture, however, and he was not entirely pleased at the arrangement, as it turned out. After some shuffling of personnel, Yates placed

---

*And to Chesterfield's "sister company", Invincible Pictures.

75

This is the Republic Lot as it appeared in 1931, when it was yet in possession of Mack Sennett, the "King of the Custard Pies." In 1934, after Sennett's bankruptcy, this became home of Mascot Pictures which, in turn, rented space to Chesterfield and Invincible. In 1935, Republic started operations, merged with Mascot, and took over this entire lot. Now the place is CBS Television City. [Photo courtesy of First Federal Savings, Hollywood/ Bruce Torrence, Historical Collection]

Levine at the head of the studio, and agreed to let the Monogram branch of the family go its separate way. Tobacco chomping Herbert John Yates was a decisive businessman, who changed what he organized, whenever it could be improved — or so he thought, anyway.

In a manner of speaking, Yates was walking in the footsteps of a very similar businessman, the late George Washington Hill, the moving force behind American Tobacco Company, for whom Yates was once a sales executive, and from whom he borrowed heavily in his ideas for a Hollywood business career.

Yates had transferred his talents from the tobacco trade to the film laboratory field. A mere twenty years old when he had joined the American Tobacco Company, he later left there to go with another tobacco firm, Liggett & Myers. At the outbreak of World War I, Yates went to work for Hedwig Film Laboratories, and ultimately organized a couple of film labs himself. In 1922, this led to the creation of Consolidated Film Industries*, a large laboratory which fattened considerably on the trade Poverty Row producers provided. Yates, however, was past fifty when he reached that point in his career which comes to include the Republic Pictures enterprise.

At the beginning of Republic's history, the studio's output strongly resembled the earlier Mascot firm, whose serials and features were literally the patterns from which so many of the earliest Republic releases were fashioned.

The first Republic features were released in the fall of 1935, the earliest of all being *Westward Ho* with John Wayne, released on August 19th of that year and followed shortly afterward by *Tumbling Tumbleweeds* with Gene Autry. By January of 1936, the firm had released seventeen feature pictures, six of which were westerns. It was not until the 1936 releases were readied that the studio succeeded in finishing its first serial, *Darkest Africa* with Clyde Beatty and which Republic followed with Ray "Crash" Corrigan in *Undersea Kingdom;* Robert Livingston in *The Vigilantes Are Coming;* and Mala in *Robinson Crusoe of Clipper Island,* all of which were also released in 1936.

The releases and the stars of Republic were for the most part not very impressive ones. John Wayne was an exception because he was a screen newcomer with a fair background of experience at other studios. Gene Autry was somewhat of an enigma. He had come to Hollywood late in 1933, appearing in two Ken Maynard films for Mascot soon after he arrived. His main fame at that time came strictly from phonograph record sales (particularly in the midwestern United States) and radio appearances in Chicago. It was a tenuous fame, and one which would hardly have caused major studios to bet money on Autry's future in films. However, as history has proved, he was one of Republic's most profitable stars, and it is difficult to imagine what the history of the firm would have been without him. (Autry left Republic later on in his career).

---

*The Consolidated firm still exists.

In the brief history of the Republic Pictures firm, there were many men who had a "turn at the wheel", acting as president. Left is James R. Grainger, who was president of the company from 1938. Before that, W. Ray Johnston and then Nat Levine had successively occupied the position. Of course, through all the changes Herbert J. Yates was a king pin, and after Grainger's departure, took over the chair as the Republic Company's president. [Photo courtesy of Jack Goetz/ Consolidated Film Industries]

Herbert J. Yates did not become well-known to the public early in his career, preferring as he did at first to remain behind the scenes. Instead, he publicized W. Ray Johnston and, later, Nat Levine as studio chieftains. Nonetheless, he eventually became publicly known for what had always been privately true, from the beginning of Republic's history, he had been the financial force behind the studio operation. [Photo courtesy of Consolidated Film Industries and Jack M. Goetz]

While released by Republic, **Tumbling Tumbleweeds** was actually copyrighted by Nat Levine's Mascot Pictures in 1935. When Republic was formed to absorb Mascot, Liberty and Monogram, the picture to the right was one of Republic's first releases.

One of the lobby cards issued in connection with the only western which Mascot released. While Ken Maynard was the star, this offering served to introduce Gene Autry to the screen, and was one of two Mascot films which did so. [Photo from author's collection]

The serials of Republic, while amazingly well-produced, had unimpressive casts and grew more and more top-heavy in non-entities as the TV craze spread, and caused the company to retrench in the serial field. By the time Republic's serial production finally halted, the firm had produced sixty-six of the continued-next-week entries, a large number of which were re-issued under titles other than those each had been made under* — just as it did with many of its features.

While Republic was in effect cast in the same mold as its predecessor, Mascot Pictures, and while many of its production techniques were borrowed from Mascot, it developed a clear-cut production style which came eventually to be all its own, and was hardly ever likened to the Mascot image.

Gradually, too, Republic gathered a large circle of players, directors, producers, and other personnel who could adapt to the studio's lightning-fast ways of making films.

John English, a film editor and director, was one of these. "John English was the type of director who was much like Frank Borzage — great on 'mood stuff'. I am surprised that he was as good as he was on action scenes," director Spencer Gordon Bennet said not long ago. "Republic paired him with William Witney to make many serials, because Witney could handle the action scenes, you see."

Spencer Gordon Bennet, too, was an important addition to the Republic directorial staff, rounding out a career which eventually totalled some fifty-four serials in all, stretching from the silent days of film-making.*

Bennet found the Republic firm a pleasant one for his talents, and a logical continuation of an experience which had begun with the early silent films, when action had been foremost. He joined Republic in 1941, a time when the firm's reputation in Hollywood was at its peak, and some of its best films being produced. "I started off at Republic by directing a serial called *Secret Service in Darkest Africa* which starred Rod Cameron. Republic spent money on that film. It first showed me what a wonderful studio that Republic was at which to work; they had the proper facilities for making action pictures.

"A director could change camera speeds in the middle of a scene at Republic — in other words, if one had a lot of horses coming toward the camera, he could start at 16 frames per second, then change speeds to a normal frame rate, 24 frames per second, as the riders came up to the camera and began to speak.

"Moreover, at Republic, we could turn out serials at a bewildering rate, 'cause all personnel, all the equipment were geared to that fast pace production style. Everyone whom Republic placed in the serial productions, for instance — assistant directors, cameramen, sound engineers, and others — were capable of doing the work under pressure, doing maybe forty or more 'set ups' per working day.

---

*Republic eventually re-issued many of its serials to television, having re-edited them to feature length. The serials, however, do not lend themselves to such editing because there are often inconsistencies in continuity which go unnoticed in a continued film, but are plainly apparent in a feature version.

---

*Bennet did some co-directing of Pearl White's serials, but was not credited with such work.

"You can't make serials at a leisurely pace, that's all there is to it. A serial director just can't say 'cut' — now let's see! — I think Republic serials gave viewers a fast action world because they were made in a fast action studio.

"I used to get home from Republic at night after six o'clock, and go right to bed after dinner, so I would be able to get up at four in the morning and study the script to ascertain in advance what camera angles were to be used, etc., — which called for really detailed knowledge of the locations to be used, as you can imagine."

In recalling Republic's policy of film production, director Spencer Gordon Bennet spoke of the actors who worked in the films made by that studio. "When we made a production for Republic, we employed players whom we could hire for a low price, but who were the best we could obtain for the money, in order to assure us of peak production for each dollar spent."

At Republic, Bennet liked the break-neck atmosphere. "It was a studio which made primarily films dealing with action and making them well.

"Around Hollywood, there is a story about how Republic once sent a film over to Fox to screen, because Republic was proud of the picture and its big sets. The story continues that Fox officials were indeed impressed with the sets, but asked where the actors were — only to be told that Republic started each morning so early that production sometimes began before the actors arrived. It may have seemed that Republic was that harried, so lightning fast were the studio's production techniques!

"The miniature department at Republic was a marvel," recalled director Spencer Gordon Bennet not long ago. "Two boys named Lydecker made up some really marvelous miniatures which added much to our Republic serials.

"The miniature department, in turn, was augmented by Republic's staff of cameramen, men such as Reggie Lanning, who could light a set in just twenty minutes, instead of the three hours that most major studios felt was necessary!

"Now don't get me wrong about the efficiency at Republic," Bennet cautioned. "There was always a good-natured atmosphere, and a large amount of kidding on the sets, but that never was allowed to interfere with production.

"In fact, we dealt with action scenes involving a lot of stunting, which called for intense concentration by everyone concerned — and which often didn't permit retakes, as in the cases where an entire set would be demolished for some fight scene. It was exacting stunting, and demanding."

"I remember that at one time *Life Magazine* was doing an article on me," stuntman David Sharpe recounted to this author recently, "they researched and got up to 3,000 pictures I'd appeared in, and they quit. You see, there were times at Republic, for instance, where you'd go on the lot and in one day work in four shows. You'd jump into one show, do some doubling in a girl's outfit, then turn around and do the same business for some actor in another show, and so on.

"And I was just one of the stuntmen at Republic. Dale Van Sickel, and several others all worked there.

Doubling for actor Clayton Moore, stuntman/player David Sharpe makes a flying leap for the purpose of saving the life of lovely Kay Aldridge. The scene is from the Republic serial **Perils of Nyoka,** *which the firm later re-issued as* **Nyoka and the Tigermen.** [*Photo courtesy of Erwin Dumbrille*]

In 1943, when Monogram Pictures produced **Two Fisted Justice**, the Hollywood stuntman David Sharpe [left] was yet appearing as a featured player. The stagecoach driver is Kermit Maynard. [Photo courtesy of Jan Barfoed]

Vera Hruba Ralston as she appeared in the Republic feature **Fair Wind to Java** [1953] in which she co-starred with Fred MacMurray.

Born in Prague, Czechoslovakia, Miss Ralston came to the United States in 1938. Subsequently her romance with Herbert Yates, Republic Pictures chieftain, caused numerous complaints among the firm's stockholders, who charged that Miss Ralston was not a money-making screen personality, though Yates continued to star her in lavish productions in spite of her lack of audience appeal. [Photo courtesy of Ted Lydecker]

The immensity of Republic's
"Mabel Normand Sound Stage"
may be imagined from this
construction photo, made during
World War II, when many persons
questioned just how it was, with
building material at a severe
premium, Mr. Yates could obtain so
much of it!

It may have ended up as Republic's
film storage vault, but the Mabel
Normand Sound Stage was once an
immense monument to Republic's
growth and determination — just
prior to the years when the spread
of television wiped out the studio.

"I don't think that at any time any one of us specialized in one particular type of stunt. We all just did what was called for by the script. For example, I've done all sorts of aircraft work, all manner of horse stunts, wrecked wagons, turned over cars, smashed planes and motor boats."

David Sharpe's nonchalant attitude toward his work as a stuntman makes his remarkable motion pictures seem almost prosaic. To legions of film goers, however, his carefully calculated stunts made up many of the most exciting moments in the films of Poverty Row, and those of Republic, in particular.

Such every-day-action-films tended often to mask the World War II-era intrigue which all too often became foremost in publicity at Republic — most of it occasioned by the romantic pecadilloes of Yates and the Czechoslovakian skating star, Vera Hruba Ralston.

"I didn't know Herbert Yates too well," Bennet continued his commentary on Republic. "Of course, one just couldn't work at the studio and not hear gossip, including comments about how one stage was simply given over to an ice skating rink which, when not used for Vera Ralston's films, was a private skating rink for Herbert Yates and Vera Ralston. In fact, a later battle by Republic stockholders was occasioned by Yates interesting concessions to Miss Ralston, as I recall."

Other of the operational aspects of Republic studios brought raised eyebrows, among which was the manner the gigantic "Mabel Normand Sound Stage" was permitted to be built during World War II, when building materials were exceedingly scarce, and when civilian construction projects were at a premium.

"Republic got permission from certain officials of the U. S. Government," one Republic executive now recalls, "to build that stage, because the government officials were given to understand that Armed Forces training films would be made there. Well, it wasn't quite that way, and I believe a lawsuit developed."

But the World War II years at Republic were dominated by actress Vera Ralston, because she was the girl friend — later the wife of Herbert Yates.

"Her films just didn't make any money and the minority stockholders at Republic finally raised hell," one ex-Republic employee says now. "After all, Vera Hruba Ralston was a large woman, who really didn't look graceful on ice skates. A Czechoslovakian skating champion she may have been, but over here in the United States she just wasn't any screen competition for Sonja Henie."

In spite of the unwiseness which Yates exhibited in the case of Miss Ralston and her films, the studio operation made a great deal of money, and some very profitable pictures, enough to mark the firm as the top studio of its kind in all Hollywood.

Over the years that it functioned, Republic made outstanding westerns which alternately featured John Wayne (who made a number of high budget non-westerns there too), Gene Autry, Roy Rogers, Don "Red" Barry, Bob Steele, Max Terhune, Smiley Burnette and many others.

In the "cornball" comedy field, the studio turned out many well-made, unpretentious features which starred Judy Canova, The Weaver Brothers and Elviry, Roy Acuff, and so on. Of that group of features, the Juda Canova films alone were for a time tremendously popular, especially when produced in "Trucolor" or "Super Cinecolor."

The studio never worked to advantage in the area of film making that was so near and dear to the hearts of officials at the Universal lot — that is, the area of the horror films. In its career, however, Republic did offer some fairly exciting mysteries and horror films, among them several which starred Erich Von Stroheim. Even Vera Hruba Ralston starred in one such film, *Murder in the Music Hall* which director John English guided well. Such features were,

For a time, Judy Canova [left] was "queen of the hillbillies" at the Republic lot. Her features — some of which co-starred comedian Joe E. Brown—eventually metamorphosed into color offerings. Her "Florida cracker type" of humor found wide appeal with the audiences who were "out there in the hinterlands" and to whom Republic features appealed. [Photo from author's collection]

Less sophicated audiences of the era around World War II enjoyed many low-budget features of this type, all of which were specially tailored to the "country and western" trade. Designed for the lower half of a double feature program, films like this one were profitable for Republic, since they were low cost productions, shot in one week or less.

In an effort to meet the television monster with some "star power," John Wayne was cast by Republic in 1951, in **The Quiet Man**, which was directed by John Ford. Co-starred with Wayne were his old friends Victor McLaglen and Maureen O'Hara. Like **MacBeth** [Orson Welles], **The Red Pony** [Robert Mitchum] and other top-budget Republic releases of the post-World War II era, however, **The Quiet Man** came along too late to save the Republic firm.

Two cowboys who discovered pure gold on the side streets of Hollywood. Gene Autry [shown above in a scene from the 1942 Republic feature **Home in Wyomin'**] entered films as a radio singer who'd come to fame via a show emanating from Chicago. His first screen appearances were in a serial **The Phantom Empire** and a Ken Maynard western, **In Old Santa Fe**, both made by Mascot. Later, when Mascot merged with Republic, Autry joined the new studio.

Roy Rogers [whose real name is Leonard Slye] came from a town near Cincinnati, Ohio. He'd never been west of the Mississippi River when he entered films. The scene below is from **Heart of the Rockies.** With Rogers is Rand Brooks. [Photo courtesy of Jan Barfoed]

Occasionally, Republic released material made by firms or producers who were not per se Republic's own. One such release was the novelty film **Bill and Coo** [1948] which, while made on the Republic lot, was independently made by comedian Ken Murray. A color feature with a cast of love birds, the miniature sets for this feature were made by the Lydeckers, the men responsible for the miniatures and many of the effects in Republic serials and features.

Olsen and Johnson made their biggest hit picture for Universal, where they appeared in **Hellzapoppin** (which was made from their Broadway show) but it was at Republic that they made some of their earliest screen appearances. Here the two comics are on the Republic lot ready to start on the production titled **All Over Town** released on September 8, 1937. (Photo courtesy of John Stransky Jr.)

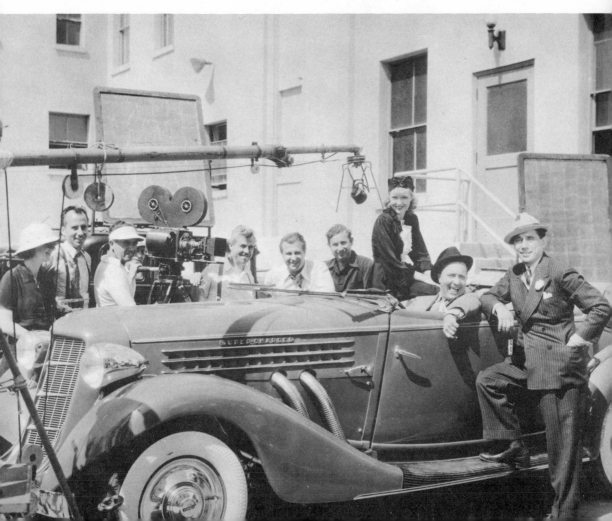

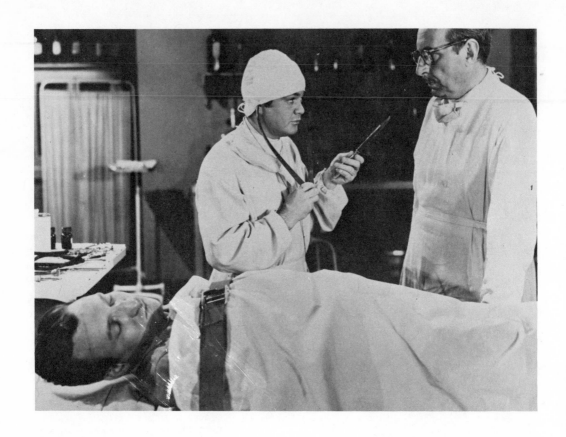

This post-war offering in the long stream of Bowery Boys features was one called **Spook Busters** [1947]. Shown here with Leo Gorcey and Huntz Hall is one of Hollywood's most famous "villains," Douglas Dumbrille. [Photo courtesy of Erwin Dumbrille]

however, exceptions at Republic Studios.

Aside from its continuing series of chapter plays, Republic seldom dabbled in the field of short subjects, a notable exception occurring during World War II, when the firm offered a series of color cartoons which featured "Charlie Horse" — and an advanced drawing technique. After the release of several such films, however, Republic left the short subject field except for its release of serials, as was noted.

When one scans the Republic history, it is in the production of serials and westerns that the firm really dominates. It is wisely remembered for pictures of these types, with some lesser recollections of the many "Republic Specials" down through the years, among them — The Fighting Kentuckian, The Quiet Man, The Fighting Seabees, and Sands of Iwo Jima, all of which starred John Wayne. Also The Red Pony with Robert Mitchum, and some of the other slick glossy musical westerns in which Gene Autry and, later, Roy Rogers starred — those atrocious "western musicals" which ultimately brought both men immense wealth.

Oddly, while Autry was indeed a Texan by birth, he had made his initial public appearance and impact in the midwest where Roy Rogers (whose real name is the commonplace Leonard Slye) was born. Both represented the kind of western feature that eventually almost totally replaced the earlier "hell for leather" cowboy films, and certainly proved the more profitable, in spite of their relatively high production costs.

By the time World War II ended, Republic had passed its peak of highly profitable productivity. In the early 1940's, the company had developed a triple-threat for the nation's box-offices: John Wayne "specials" for prestige; Autry (and later Roy Rogers) for the singing westerns; and finally, the "Saturday Matinee" serials — all three types of films tremendous money makers. Everything else in Republic's repertoire ran strictly second to these three phases of film making — even the color features with Judy Canova, Forrest Tucker, and the like.

And in spite of the fact that the company saw some abrupt changes in their output — the loss of Gene Autry, first to the Armed Forces, then to his own production outfit, which released through Columbia, then to television; then a gradual diminution of John Wayne's services to the Republic label, culminating in John Ford's Technicolor feature The Quiet Man (1952); and a gradual loss of audience interest in westerns and serials, it appeared that Republic might gradually make the transition to the output of top-budget films, and even a TV series or two. That transition never occurred, and Republic became only an office, which carried on mainly the business of releasing Republic's old product to television.

The vast Republic studio was sold to CBS and became that firm's "CBS Television City." So the great hollowness of the Mabel Normand Sound Stage came to know the strange immediacy of television which, once the device arrived in Hollywood, had obliterated so much of the motion picture's greatness.

One of a large number of the well-made series which offered audiences John Wayne [who assayed a role in the series only for a short time]. This presentation is typical of the western offerings which issued from the Republic Firm.

Just prior to World War II, John Wayne was still appearing in "B" pictures, such as this one, **Overland Stage Raiders**, [1938] one of the well remembered **Three Mesquiteers** series. Wayne's partners are Ray Corrigan [left] and Max Terhune. But a few years later Wayne starred in such Republic "Class A" features as, **The Fighting Seabees**, and was on his way to real stardom and to becoming one of Republic's top moneymakers.

The Johnny Mack Brown western **Trail of Vengeance** was released through Republic Pictures soon after that firm was organized in 1935. The picture was, however, produced by an outside production unit, that of A. W. Hackel, who earlier had released such films through his own organization Supreme Pictures. [Photo courtesy of Jan Barfoed]

One of the first deluxe westerns to be made by Republic was **The Dark Command** starring John Wayne, Walter Pidgeon and Claire Trevor. Shown here are two scenes from this offering. John Wayne is easily recognizable in the above action scene and Walter Pidgeon is vividly portrayed in the picture below.

An Anemic Phoenix Rises

IN the summer of 1939, Ben Judell placed a two page ad in *Box Office,* an exhibitor trade publication, containing in part the following: "Art and delayed tempo production have their place, to be sure, but millions of theatre goers, on whom exhibitors depend for steady profitable patronage, steadfastly refuse to pay for anything except moving pictures."

His timing was perfect on this ad, for several reasons. Grand National's future was uncertain, clouded by bankruptcy and impending foreclosure. Meanwhile, Republic was taking the first big step into major productions with the hiring of Raoul Walsh from Warner Brothers to direct a large scale western about Quantrell's Raiders starring John Wayne and Claire Trevor. *The Dark Command,* followed by *Four Faces West*, again with John Wayne and Francis Dee, elevated Republic to a status of a "minor" among "majors." Monogram, at the same time, was growing and had opened more film exchanges which it owned and operated. But perhaps the most important reason of all for the right timing, was that the "States Right" market was drying up. And with only Sam Katzman producing westerns under his Victory banner, along with a handful of westerns from Harry S. Webb's Metropolitan Pictures and the Alexander Brothers producing some Ken Maynard westerns from their Colony Pictures Company, this was a welcome announcement.

The "States Right" exchanges needed pictures to distribute to the small independent theatres, which in turn, needed pictures in order to keep their theatres open. So it was no surprise then, when distributor and exhibitor alike, rallied to the support, with pledges of bookings and financial backing for Ben Judell and his newly formed Producers Distributing Corporation, which was dedicated to high entertainment and exploitation values.

Ben Judell was by no means a newcomer to the distribution field. He was manager of the Mutual Film Exchanges in Milwaukee, Wisconsin, where Mutual was well known for their Chaplin comedies. Then, in 1917, Judell became an independent film distributor for he knew the market and marketing procedures for the product he would furnish. He knew his first move was to rally enough distributor support, which in turn, would lead to pledges of bookings and, with collateral, would secure enough financing to get PDC's program off the ground.

Ben Judell, just a year before, had produced some exploitation pictures for the "States Right" market through his Progressive Pictures Corporation. Dealing solely in exploitation pictures under such titles as *Rebellious Daughters, Delinquent Parents* and *Slander House,* these pictures did well enough for the market intended, and made the name Judell a familiar one to the exhibitors.

PDC's initial program was to be three

series of westerns, eight pictures to a series. The first was heralded as "Tales of Billie The Kid" with George Houston playing the role of the legendary rebel. His exhibitor trade ads on this series made interesting reading by themselves. After all, what film booker could resist such copy as: "Based on the career of the Southwest's most misunderstood character who wrote his laws on curtains of gunfire with bullets of flaming lead."

His second announced series was to star the steel-eyed sharpshooter — Tim McCoy: "A star now at the zenith of a glorious screen career, with millions of loyal fans. These are investments, not speculations," proclaimed the ad.

The third series was, and this is the most curious of all, to star a western family with a juvenile to carry the lead. M-G-M had their successful Hardy family; 20th Century Fox's "B" Unit had their answer to the Hardy Family with a real-life family — James Gleason, wife Lucille, and son Russell with Harry Davenport portraying the grandfather. So riding on the crest of the popular trend of family series, PDC would produce a western family series known as the "Sagebrush Family". It was to be a "family series that upsets traditions and pleases everyone in the household." The copywriter must have run out of steam from this rather ambiguous description of the Sagebrush Family. Perhaps it would be safe to assume that the concept of this series hadn't been fully developed by press time.

Concept or not, the machinery of PDC was set into motion. A later announcement in the trade publications attested to this activity with a budget of one million dollars, which represented their program for the 1939-1940 season. However, this program was

soon to be announced, expanded from 36 to 60 pictures! And the amount of money allocated for investment into production was considerably raised as well.

Judell placed Sigmund Neufeld in charge of western production at PDC. Neufeld had already earned himself a niche as a successful western producer with Puritan Pictures and their Tim McCoy westerns, and the highly successful Northwest Mounted Police westerns starring Kermit Maynard at Ambassador-Conn Pictures.

Besides Neufeld, six associate producers were signed to carry out the program while distribution agreements were being arranged with twelve exchanges. So, the groundwork was set for one of the most ambitious independent production organizations to appear on the independent scene since the founding of Republic.

By August of 1939, Judell had assigned Sherman Scott, Robert Tansey, Peter Stewart and Victor Halperin to directional contracts. In addition to the three western series, two exploitation subjects were added to the production slate, *Torture Ship,* which Victor Halperin would direct, and *Hitler, Beast of Berlin.* At this time, the Nazi theme was untouched by Hollywood producers. However, Warner Brothers had just released *Confessions of a Nazi Spy* which was doing an unbelievable business. So Judell, wanting to cash in on the success of *Nazi Spy,* rushed his project into production.

Meanwhile, PDC was going ahead with its three series of previously announced westerns. But now Judell planned on expanding the company. To produce the westerns in Arizona, land was purchased near Prescott in order to

construct sound stages and a western street and also for an administration building. Peter Stewart would supervise this phase of the expansion under the plans of art director Fred Preble.

Another two page ad was inserted in *Box Office* to publicize this move. It read somewhat like a travel folder: "Westerns have outgrown Hollywood, so we are shooting ours in Arizona. Romantic Arizona, one of the last settled of the frontier states, just as it appeared to the trail-blazing 49'ers — two-gun badmen and the pioneers who risked the scalping knives of savage indian redskins to carve a great State out of the wilderness. All of this magnificence will be ours!" What exhibitor, catering to a western buying audience could resist booking such a program of pictures as PDC promised to deliver?

Although the United States was still neutral, our sympathies were with the Allies in their struggle against Hitler, for the Nazi take-over of Europe had begun. The world was divided and at war. Universal had reissued its anti-war film, *All Quiet on the Western Front* with a foreword by Carl Laemmle calling for mankind to realize the horrors of war and not to again make the mistakes of World War I. It was a noble but futile gesture.

In September, Judell decided to upgrade *Hitler, Beast of Berlin* to a 90-minute "A" picture budget. It was held back in production at the Fine Arts Lot (Grand National).

(While this was occurring, *Sagebrush Family Trails West* was shooting in Arizona. Bobby Clark, a youthful rodeo champion, and trick rider Ken Duncan, were in the cast.)

Two weeks later, *Hitler, Beast of Berlin* was set into production. Sherman Scott who had directed several of the Time documentaries for Louis DeRochemont in New York was then chosen to direct. Roland Drew, Steffi Duna, Vernon Dent and Alan Ladd in his first screen appearance, made up the new cast.

Once in production, and to counteract any industry uncertainty and apprehension about the *Beast of Berlin* project, Judell reiterated to the exhibitors that his film would deal with the underground anti-Nazi war movement, not be war propaganda, and was not intended to inspire a hatred for any European political group. A typical Judell publicity release stated that it was

One of the unsung motion picture events of 1939 was the release of Producers Pictures Corporation's feature **Goose Step** *— later retitled as shown in the photo above. It was one of Alan Ladd's first screen appearances, and united him with such veteran performers as Greta Granstedt, Steffi Duna, and Lucien Littlefield. [Photo courtesy of Erwin Dumbrille]*

going to be "action on all fronts, war or no war."

Daily chartered flights were set up between Prescott, Arizona and Hollywood for processing and printing of the shooting location film works. Three more productions went before the cameras: *Buried Alive* with Beverly

Roberts and Robert Wilcox; *Mercy Plane* with James Dunn and Frances Gifford, and *Invisible Killer.* When October rolled around, the Arizona studio was scheduled to open in a big way. Governor R. T. Jones would be attending and there was to be a street parade and barbeque on opening day.

Back in California, *Hitler, Beast of Berlin* was rushed through post-production by film editor Holbrook Todd. Two months later, the picture was reviewed by the *Box Office* film reviewer. A phenomenal job to accomplish in such a short time. Soon after, a reviewer commented "that it was a timely picture, filmed with the realization of what was happening in Germany. The story concerned itself with a small band of National Socialists, in which Roland Drew is a guiding force figure. They are apprehended and thrown into a concentration camp — suffering and abuse are inevitable. They ultimately escape and flee to Switzerland where they continue to fight for freedom of the German people."

By November, the picture was put into general release and PDC production money was now tied up in seven pictures and the construction of a location studio in Arizona. However, an unforeseen chain reaction of adverse events were beginning to unfold — CENSORSHIP!

Certain states had censor boards and only three of these, thus far, had approved the picture — Michigan, Pennsylvania and New York. New York, however, wanted the name Hitler deleted from the title. This meant recalling of the prints circulated in that state and having replacements manufactured with the title *Beast of Berlin.* The war still had not hit close enough to home and some areas felt the picture

was offensive to the Germans as indicated when the censor boards of Chicago and Providence turned the picture down completely for it still had not been granted a Production Seal by the Motion Picture Association. Lacking Hayes office approval, the picture *Beast of Berlin* was suffering from being barred by the larger producer-controlled theatre circuits. Furthermore, an organized opposition to the showing of the picture was mounting. Judell finally got the Hayes office approval and Seal of Approval when he agreed to drop the title *Hitler, Beast of Berlin.* The prints were all recalled again and the title changed to *Goose Step.*

So much for the domestic release — which in some instances only serves to enable the producer to break even on their investment — for profit is realized from the foreign markets. In the case of *Goose Step,* however, foreign acceptance was slow. A new flow of cash was looked for, if, and when *Goose Step* was passed by the English censors in England. But this did not occur. Now the lack of cash flow back to the producer began to take its toll.

By February 1940, Pathe Laboratories was holding a lien of $90,000 in uncollected receipts invested in a seven picture program by Judell. At this point, Producers Distributing Corporation would have gone into bankruptcy court, the assets to be auctioned off to pay the creditors, and another chapter would have closed on Poverty Row — but a curious event took place.

The distributors that held "States Right" franchises for Producers Distributing Corporation releases, asked Pathe Laboratories not to foreclose on Ben Judell's company. The distributors instead, were asked to contribute to the production costs, and to the payment of previous debts. And so, in March of 1940, a new company was formed by the creditors. Adhering to their determination to keep the company in operation, Sigmund Neufeld Productions was formed to succeed Producers Distributing Corporation. Ben Judell was relieved of his company, went back to the midwest and resumed active operation of his own circuit of independent film exchanges. In the three months existence of his company, Ben Judell had produced seven pictures, built a studio in Arizona and spent over a million dollars. And now, nine months later, from his initial announcement in Box Office, everything had vanished.

The new company was backed by Robert S. Benjamin, attorney for Pathe Laboratories, and the various franchise distributors comprised the balance of the company. This interim organization, reorganized as Sigmund Neufeld Productions, moved into high gear with the announcement of a modest, realistic 15-picture program for the balance of 1940. Neufeld's revised production schedule was divided among seven melodramas, four Bob Steele westerns, and four Tim McCoy westerns.

The first picture put into production was one that teamed James Dunn and Frances Gifford in a fast-moving and breezy sort of "B" melodrama that became the formula for countless "programmers" of the 1940's. The Box Office trade reviewer had the following comment about Hold That Woman: "Comedy-drama in a glib sort of way is the general tone of this story of skip tracers — investigators of people who try to beat out installment companies and collectors . . ."

The releases of this successor company were gaining in theatre bookings and audience acceptance — one such production being The Devil Bat. Directed by Jean Yarbrough, this story centered around an evil scientist developing a shaving lotion which he gave to his intended victims, then released a giant bat which was attracted to the shaving lotion. Dave O'Brien played a quick-witted reporter who figured it all out.

Exhibitor support continued to mount for the company, as indicated by one showman's comments to Box Office in the "Exhibitor Has His Say" section of the publication (regarding Marked Men with Warren Hull and Isabel Jewell): "A fairly good prison story and the acting not too bad. Sound not so good. However, PRC is trying hard to deliver, so give them a break they so justly deserve."

November 1940, saw the interim production organization of Sig Neufeld reorganized as Producers Releasing Corporation. Harry Rathner was president briefly — then in December of that same year, O. Henry Briggs was appointed as the new head of PRC. (Briggs had been head of Pathe Laboratories and Kenneth Young was the chairman of the Pathe board). Under new management, $150,000 in additional financing was secured.

Production was scheduled to gorge ahead under the supervision of George Batchelor, who in the early 1930's headed up Chesterfield Pictures for the eight years of life of that organization. During the last four years with Chesterfield, Batchelor was associated with Maury Cohen in the administration of Invincible Pictures.

The PRC company, under Batchelor, was set up with five unit production chiefs: Guy Thayer, Jed Budell, Ted

Ex-swimming champion Buster Crabbe [right] played in a long series of westerns issuing from the PRC firm. Above is a scene from a 1944 offering titled, **Valley of Vengeance**. At left is Steve Clark. The comic sidekick is Al "Fuzzy" St. John. [Photo courtesy of Jan Barfoed]

Al "Fuzzy" St. John, George Houston, and Dennis Moore in a publicity still from the 1942 PRC western, **The Lone Rider in Border Roundup**. [Photo courtesy of Jan Barfoed]

PRC/Eagle Lion offered this 1947 western with Eddie Dean and Roscoe Ates. [Photo courtesy of Jan Barfoed]

Richmont, Sigmund Neufeld and E. B. Derr. However, not all production units were housed in the Fine Arts Studio,* but instead were located at various rental location studios about Hollywood.

Jed Budell's first picture produced under the PRC banner over at the Talisman Studio was a most curious one. Budell seemed to prefer comedy and treated his subjects with comedy overtones. *Misbehaving Husbands,* however, was an outright comedy, which starred Harry Langdon and the silent screen star, Betty Blythe of *She* and *The Queen of Sheba.*

In the 1941 production season, the Tim McCoy westerns were dropped while the lead of Billy the Kid was changed from Bob Steele to Buster Crabbe. Later, a new western series was added with George Houston, a rugged looking actor with a good singing voice who was cast as the Lone Rider. Of the first entry into this new series, *Lone Rider Rides On,* a trade reviewer felt compelled to comment: "First in this series is strictly routine without particular distinction. The music saves it. It is played loud and long. Obviously a rush job as some scenery is shot in overcast weather."

This 1941-1942 season was a frantic one for Hollywood. From 528 to 547 pictures were planned by Hollywood

*Formerly the Grand National and before that the Educational Studios.

*A scene from PRC's offering of **Corregidor** — a motion picture which was destined to lead the way to new war thrillers, those based upon actual events in history. The girl is Elissa Landi and the man Rick Vallin.*

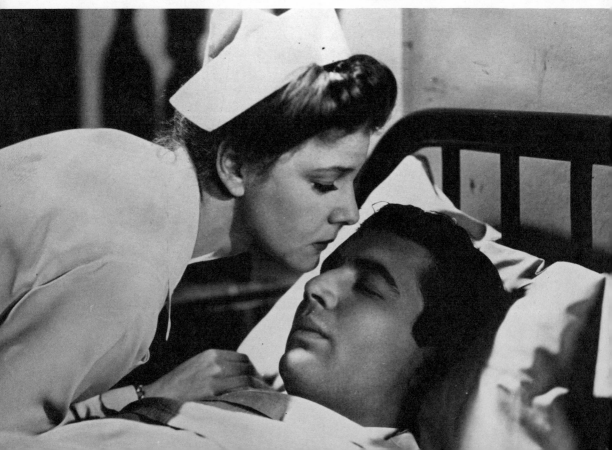

producers. (Films were needed for morale and entertainment in the military as well as on the home front). Under George Batchelor's supervision, PRC produced 44 pictures during this season — some bad, but in the company of some sleepers which were exceedingly good.

When the productions were bad, the trade reviewers were never hesitant to take PRC to task. In a Roger Pryor and Virginia Vale spy melodrama, *South of Panama*, they were most caustic in the *Box Office* trade comment: "Very little imagination, too much talk and an overworked idea aren't exactly virtues leading into entertainment. There is questionable taste in dedicating the film to the RAF just because the plot tumbles over a secret paint formula for planes and some misplaced aerial maneuver stock footage."

However, two producers were to come into PRC's fold who turned the attention of the industry toward the "war baby." The first was writer-producer Martin Mooney, whose stories were fresh, dialog crisp, and who put top production values on the screen, far exceeding the restrictions of his budgets. Mooney was an ex-newspaper reporter with a colorful background, including the authorship of a series of articles on gambling rackets for the New York American. (He was fined and imprisoned for refusing to give the source of his information).

The second production team was the Kozinsky Brothers. Their first picture, *Paper Bullets,* dealt with metropolitan underworld vice and corruption. It starred Jack LaRue, Joan Woodbury, and Alan Ladd. This was Ladd's second screen appearance for PRC. The picture, capably directed by Phil Rosen, was acclaimed by *Variety, Hollywood*

Reporter and *Box Office* alike: "It will undoubtedly make a significant impression on the market for which it is intended." "It stacks up favorably with efforts from the major lots which are budgeted at three or four times as many dollars." "A competent cast contributes sincere performances throughout and carry this underworld expose nicely."

Except for *Beast of Berlin, Paper Bullets* was the first PRC production to receive bookings in several large first-run theatre circuits. Fox West Coast and the Warner Theatres gave it extensive playdates.

Soon after, the Kozinsky Brothers moved over to Monogram where they became known as the King Brothers and where they produced one of that studio's biggest money making crime dramas in *Dillinger*. Laurence Tierney, brother of Scott Brady, was introduced to the screen as this lengendary vice-lord.

Meanwhile, back at PRC ranch, Buster Crabbe was pasting Charles King all over the place, as was usual in Crabbe's westerns. But having once played Tarzan in the early thirties, it seemed fitting for the studio to cash in on that image, too. So, Buster would slip into a loin cloth and do an occasional jungle story. *Jungle Man* led off a series of four "Gorilla and Girl" melodramas, which were turned out over the next few years, the other releases including *Jungle Siren*, with burlesque queen Ann Corio; *Girl and the Gorilla* and *Nabonga,* both with Julie London.

Only one trade review need be quoted which about sums it up for the entire package. *Box Office* commented about the 1941 release of *Jungle Man* thusly: "Not once during its hour's running time does it rise above mediocrity. A tootsie runs around in shorts and a sarong, but that's all the diversion. Many stock shots of lions, monkeys and snakes were thrown in to embellish the story. They don't. They hardly mean anything in the continuity. Story-wise, it is a far-fetched concoction with every indication of being written by a school-boy. Buster Crabbe is a jungle medico. An archaeological expedition comes his way, with Sheila Darcy and her pappy. The lost city seekers go off on their search. A fever epidemic strikes a native village. Crabbe needs serum. The ship carrying it sank. Crabbe recovers the stuff, returns to find Miss Darcy sick, the expedition returns minus one member. Crabbe cures the girl. Romantic fade-out."

To come up with an outstanding picture on a short budget and a two-week schedule is a tribute to the ingenuity of its producer and director. Such again, was the case of Martin Mooney. This time it was a modest budget horse racing picture, *Mr. Celebrity.* It starred the youthful Buzz Henry and Doris Day. William Beaudine directed. A reviewer observed: "Many are the racetrack pictures produced by majors at 5 to 10 times the cost, that offered less down-to-earth enter-tainment. Clara Kimball Young and Francis X. Bushman try to get their grandson from his uncle, a veterinarian who follows the track, the boy beats him by training a long shot winner."

By 1942, PRC had acquired ownership of 23 film exchanges. Moreover, a move was underway to produce fewer pictures and upgrade production values. With a heavy backlog of 80 pictures piled up in the exchanges, PRC would be able to slacken production enough to concentrate on better quality products — increased costs — better stories and additional name values. Such was the announcement made in the second annual sales convention made by President O. Henry Briggs in May, 1942.

Later, George Batchelor resigned as production supervisor and was replaced by Leon Fromkess. Sigmund Neufeld remained in charge of western production and the Fine Arts lot on 7324 Santa Monica Boulevard became the PRC studios. The "Lone Rider" series was abandoned and in its place, a "trio series" was added. Lee Powell, a favorite Republic serial hero from *The Lone Ranger,* and *Fighting Devil Dogs,* was recruited along with Art Davis and singer William "Radio" Boyd.

There were two very unusual pictures that were produced in the 1942 season, both of which received trade acceptance. Although the title, *Broadway Big Shot,* had all the sounds of a "B" picture stamped all over it, neverthe-less, it was a superior story which more than made up for a small budget and shooting schedule. This was a Jed Budell production, which William Beaudine directed. In this Martin Mooney story, Ralph Byrd plays a reporter who allows himself to be framed on a larceny rap, so he can uncover a big story from within a prison. He checks in to serve his sentence only to discover the convict he intended quizzing has died. At the same time, the governor whom he counted upon for a quick pardon has been defeated for re-election. An unusual tale, *Box Office* acclaimed it by saying the film measured up to the best PRC release to date.

In 1943, the war situation was getting critical for the Allies. Losses in the South Pacific were a disappointment to the United States. At such a time, producer Edward Finney brought an idea for a war story concerning the battle of Cor-

Ben Pivar, who's been a producer of "B" features at Universal, left that studio when Universal merged with International Pictures, and was phasing out its "B" picture schedule. One Universal film, **The Brute Man**, was brought over to PRC by Pivar and released under that trade-mark.

Rondo Hatton, whose facial deformity was caused by Elephantiasis, appeared even more grotesque in **The Brute Man** through the use of a wide-angle lens, and low-key lighting. [Photo courtesy of Erwin Dumbrille]

regidor to PRC. The result was *Corregidor* with Otto Kruger and Elissa Landi. Directed by Lew Landers, it dealt with the heroic defense of the island fortress in the Philippines. The PRC publicity department heralded it as a factual account in an authentic atmosphere. The theme conveyed the super-human efforts of doctors and nurses in caring for the sick and wounded.

Up to now, pictures with a war theme, in the industry and at PRC in particular, had only fictional characters involved in a war situation — as in *Bombs Over Burma, A Yank in Lybia, Prisoner of Japan* and *Lady From Chungking. Corregidor,* however, set a trend in the industry. The majors came out with a series of war films based on actual campaigns: *Bataan, Wake Island,* and *Guadacanal Diary.* PRC had led the way!

The output of pictures in 1943 was cut from thirty-seven to twenty-six with the budgets of those twenty-six increased and production values stressed. One reason for this action was to heighten morale during the grim war years of 1943. To do this, several light comedies and musicals were planned, which required the added production money.

The jitterbug craze was captured in the Dickie Moore musical film *Jive Junction* followed by *Harvest Melody* which was a light-hearted tuneful musical with Johnny Downs, Rosemary Lane, The Radio Rogues and Eddie LeBaron's Orchestra.

For comedy there was, *My Son, The Hero* with Patsy Kelly, Roscoe Karnes, Carol Hughes, Maxie Rosenbloom and Luis Albernio. The talents of Patsy Kelly were utilized in a follow-up release of *Danger! Women At Work.* The fun

being provided by Mary Brian, Isabel Jewell, and funnymen Warren Hyman and Vince Barnett.

In 1944, the number of releases remained the same, however the quality was upgraded even more and a greater variety of themes offered. Music and light comedy were stressed again, producing two productions which were quite successful and interesting.

Producer Leon Fromkess and associate Martin Mooney assigned John Carradine and Jean Parker to the very wordy, though tense, *Bluebeard.* This periodic picture, set in the 1890's necessitated costumes and special sets which posed a thorny budget consideration. To do the film on limited money, the sets were small, to be sure, but built with forced perspective, an economy particularly evident in the rooftop chase sequence, which climaxed the picture. Director Edgar Ulmer as well as the performances of Carradine and Parker were first rate.

A second picture produced by Fromkess dealt with the American family during wartime. James Lydon was the returning serviceman in *When the Lights Go On Again.* An amnesia victim as a result of a war injury, his adjustment to civilian life was dramatic. The use of the popular war-theme song, from which the title was taken, made it a touching film.

A change of pace was later in store for James Lydon in *The Town Went Wild.* Lydon and Freddie Bartholomew were neighbors and best friend sons of feuding fathers. They share the same birth date. When Freddie decides to marry Lydon's sister, it is discovered that the babies were switched in the hospital at birth, and boy's birth certificates confused. The court orders them to switch back to their rightful parents and the comedy complications became hilarious. The film was a creditable job to writer-producers Bernard Roth, Clarence Green and Russell Rouse and director Ralph Murphy.

The year 1944 was rounded out with the one unique picture that garnered critical approval. *Minstrel Man* starring vaudeville performer Benny Fields with Gladys George as his wife, caused PRC to pour its all-time highest budget into this production.

"In story, cast, production values, performance, music, director and other departments, the picture transcends anything that has heretofore borne the PRC trademark," proclaimed the *Box Office* reviewer.

A melodrama, it was reminiscent of something that Al Jolson might have done years before, using the same dramatic ingredients of pathos, and telling the story of a minstrel while wisely avoiding most of the cliches that enter into films of a theatrical background. Most of the songs were original, but one standard was incorporated, "Melancholy Baby." Nat Levine's former Mascot film editor, Joseph Lewis, directed.

At the same time, psychological characters and low-key moods were used to full advantage in *Fog Island* with that grand character actor, Lionel Atwill, co-starring with Veda Ann Borg. Besides *Fog Island*, Leon Fromkess turned out another unique picture that year, in *Detour*. Fromkess and his associate Martin Mooney offered one of PRC's finest "B" pictures. It had all the quality and solid performances on a par with any of the slick programmers that RKO was turning out in the 1940's and 1950's. The *Box Office* film review spoke of *Detour* as being "a praiseworthy job of picture making any major studio could proudly place its trademark. A tense, suspenseful gripping drama, the picture is exceptionally well-written, produced and directed by Edgar Ulmer — but its greatest asset is a pair of outstanding performances by Tom Neal and Ann Savage. No reason why it could not find important bookings in theatres which normally show PRC products.

Tom Neal plays a hitch-hiker whom fate confronts with a situation in which he appears guilty of murder. In running away from the circumstantial evidence, he inadvertently commits another slaying. His fight with conscience and his apprehension are intensely dramatic."

One final release which came out of PRC's 1945 season which was a "sleeper" that caught on and did phenomenal business was *The Enchanted Forest*. It all began when producer Jack Schwartz assigned director Lew Landers to this project. On the PRC set, between stages 1 and 2, there was a sliding sound-proofed wall which, when rolled open, resulted in one huge sound stage. It was here that an interior "green" set was constructed — a decision which was further enhanced by photographing the picture in Cinecolor. Edmund Lowe, Brenda Joyce and Harry Davenport were cast in the picture.

One critic wrote of the film: "Adults will enjoy every moment of its pine-scented charm; youngsters will thrill to each furry or feathered creature in the picture and youths from six to sixty will project themselves longingly into the leading masculine characters. The story is that of a baby, separated from its mother in a train wreck, and brought up· as a child of nature by animals and a kindly hermit. A romance between the

The "old hermit" in **Enchanted Forest** who lived in a hollow redwood tree was veteran actor Harry Davenport, who was a completely believable, delightfully lovable, leading character.

This still photo from **Enchanted Forest** portrays all but one of the cast. Pictured above are Edmund Lowe, Brenda Joyce, Billy Severn, John Litel [standing] and the seemingly intelligent police dog.

Brenda Joyce and Edmund Lowe added their charm to the PRC feature **Enchanted Forest**. At the time that this film was produced [1945] Lowe already was well past fifty; however, he made a handsome and suave leading man for this gem from Poverty Row.

This is a publicity picture made for use with the PRC 1945 Cinecolor offering, **The Enchanted Forest**, one of the best-made of all that studio's films.

widowed mother and a physician and the depredations of a lumber tycoon form effective counterplots. Lew Landers directed with patience and understanding."

The average running time of a "B" picture ranged from 55 to 75 minutes. (The shorter running time made a film suitable for double billing). However, *The Enchanted Forest* was 84 minutes in running time, which meant that in single billing situations, the picture had to be strong enough to stand alone on its own merits.

The Enchanted Forest received bookings in all of the largest theatre circuits throughout the country. It opened in Times Square at the Victoria Theatre. (It was the successful employment of the Cinecolor process in this film, which prompted several major studios to employ the color). The film received considerable attention and critical acclaim. One reviewer described it as a Disney movie come to life. (This was before Disney abandoned animation for cheaper live action photography). Later, this theme was picked up by the publicity department of PRC and incorporated into the catch-line copy for their newspaper ads and pressbooks.

In a move to upgrade the image of the company, the name PRC was buried in 1949. A joint releasing arrangement with Arthur Rank in England resulted in the absorption of PRC by the newly-formed Eagle-Lion international firm.

Then in 1950, Film Classics Pictures merged with Eagle-Lion and for a brief time the new company was known as Eagle-Lion Classics. Finally, in 1951, Arthur Krim, within two months after taking over as president of United Artists, effected a merger with Eagle-Lion. The purchase price being $500,000 plus 5% of the gross of the David Lear film *Oliver Twist* which Eagle-Lion was distributing at that time.

William Heineman and Max Young-stein were placed in charge of domestic distribution and advertising, publicity and exploitation, respectively, and by this merger, continued the operation, giving United Artists a definite "tie-in" with Eagle-Lion.

Thus, ironically, did Poverty Row's PRC Pictures, metamorphose into a firm which, in turn, was swallowed up by one of the majors. Oddly, it was a bit of legerdemain which even Herbert J. Yates was unable to accomplish with the Republic organization, and a trick which Allied Artists (as an outgrowth of Monogram) only partly succeeded in carrying out with the word $UCCE$$. Few film outfits can pick up their chips and walk away so successfully.

Serials and Westerns
From Gower Gulch

IF the "shoestring" film producers of yesteryear had any two staples which were their bread and butter, these were the serials and westerns. Both types were quite readily marketed, and moreover, were low budget films of standardized storyfare. These attributes gave such entries considerable appeal to Poverty Row film makers, who revered economy and a guaranteed return on their investment in each film.

After all, there was no use in attempting a high budget film, a glamor type of production, down in the less-prosperous neighborhoods of Hollywood, for even if the necessary budget and the stars for such a film could be found, almost no independent producer who released his films outside the eight major labels could market such a picture.*

Realizing this, most of the producers who worked in the shadow of the major studios restricted themselves to features and serials which had their tap roots in action, intrigue, adventure and mystery. Only occasionally did they attempt anything different from these. A few moments perusal of the illustrations in this book will indicate the diversity of such productions.

It is true that some of the Poverty Row producers shied away from the western and the serial, but such organizations almost invariably remained in the "B" budget film category, producing modest unassuming films designed to be one-half of a double feature program in somewhat less than plushy theatres. Indeed, the U.S. market in the 1930's to 1950's was divided sharply into one "exclusive group" of large theatres, which usually did not even present any films made by independent studios* and another which presented "subsequent runs" of major films, often paired with an offering from Povery Row. Films designated as independent and major productions for use in "double bills" usually had a running time of not more than 70-80 minutes.

As for the serials of Hollywood, they were restricted sharply to the few neighborhood theatres which possessed a constant repeat trade from their given areas, and thus could afford and benefit financially from the week after week return of the same patrons. A handful of large "downtown" theatres utilized the episode plays, too, but these were the exception rather than being part of an accepted formula.

As for the western features of the "B" variety, these were almost always the

---

*Grand National bankrupted itself releasing such a production and Republic did not fare well with "prestige" pictures, either.

*There were some noteworthy exceptions. Republic had rather good luck in getting features like The Quiet Man with John Wayne into the cushy downtown theatres ... PRC with its color feature The Enchanted Forest, but these were remarkable exceptions.

MAN WITH THE STEEL WHIP

A REPUBLIC SERIAL IN 12 CHAPTERS

FEATURING
RICHARD SIMMONS · BARBARA BESTAR · DALE VAN SICKEL
MAURITZ HUGO · LANE BRADFORD
Written by RONALD DAVIDSON   Associate Producer and Director FRANKLIN ADREON
REPUBLIC PICTURES CORPORATION · HERBERT J. YATES, PRESIDENT

STRANGE MONSTERS INVADE THE JUNGLE!

THE MOST EXCITING SERIAL EVER FILMED!

PANTHER GIRL OF THE KONGO

A REPUBLIC SERIAL IN 12 CHAPTERS

FEATURING
PHYLLIS COATES · MYRON HEALEY · ARTHUR SPACE · JOHN DAY · MIKE RAGAN
Written by RONALD DAVIDSON · Associate Producer-Director FRANKLIN ADREON

From its first serial release **Darkest Africa** [1936] to its final one **King of the Carnival** [1955] Republic issued a total of sixty-six such pictures, a sizable volume which included some of the most slickly made of all the continued-next-week films. [Photos courtesy of Jack Jardine]

private province of the small neighborhood "grind house" i.e., the theatre which specialized in action films, and subsequent runs of major pictures.

There was no delusion among practical, hardheaded producers of Poverty Row regarding the markets for their products. They were turning out a product which at best could be sold into a restricted number of theatres, would be shunned by the large cinema palaces, and which would return an almost accurately predictable amount of money. Within these narrow confines, then — in some ways more restrictive than Poverty Row itself — some impressive and entertaining films were turned out, as well as the majority of Hollywood's western and serial offerings.

It is important that the reader know and understand these elements of independent film production, for they explain many of the limitations of productions made outside of the major studios. Moreover, they help one to realize why it is utterly foolish to compare the two diverse production entities, i.e., the major studios and the small independent operations. More importantly, though, these elements are in themselves a sort of explanation of why the many "Poverty Row" denizens and their films should not be ignored when film history is being written and should never have been ignored by the Museum of Modern Art.

Many film historians have attempted to explain the absence of "B" westerns and the serials from the production schedules of most major studios* by indicating that through some oversight,

these otherwise canny operators overlooked them. Nothing could be farther from true. Most of the established major studios had finally centered their production activities upon releases which could be played, at maximum profit, in large downtown theatres, and which hardly would be likely to utilize low cost tales of the sagebrush or serials. It was as simple as that. Such a sharp dichotomy created the small but profitable market which independent film producers sought to serve.

The independent producers could not care less whether or not audiences at Grauman's Chinese Theatre, or Broadway's Strand recognized Bob Steele; Gene Autry or Frankie Darro! The market for the films of these and many other players lay beyond the brightly lighted facades of Broadway, Hollywood Boulevard and other suburbia centers, anyway.

In these movie houses which existed on the side streets for the children and those adults who chose their film fare on the action side, Poverty Row found its greatest market. For these audiences, the cinema players and the directors who could adapt themselves to the budgets and shooting schedules which allowed little time for retakes, fared exceedingly well. It was, after all, a market which could not have been invaded successfully by the major studios, whose productions and methods were geared to a much higher priced market. Then too, most of the major studios could not fathom the vogues which the audiences of the "little theatres" were inclined to display, and moreover, did not care to learn.

Such major production circles could not really worry about how, in the period 1930-1950, distinct vogues

---

*Universal and Columbia being exceptions where serial production was concerned, and where "B" budget westerns abounded.

existed for various western players, for example, who enjoyed brief flings at "stardom" then quietly disappeared from the screen — or else settled into "character" roles. This included a number of players who had played in major features, it is true, though usually not in top budget offerings.

Through the changes of vogue among sidestreet audiences, though, there was a surprising number of players who managed to retain appeal for several generations, among them John Wayne, Bob Steele, Tim McCoy, Johnny Mack Brown, Ken Maynard, Raymond Hatton, Harry Carey, and a handful of others. Contrasting with this group, however, were many cowboy players who enjoyed relatively brief fame during these two decades which we are assaying here — including Wally Wales (Hal Taliaferro), Rex Bell, Fred Scott, Dorothy Page, "Buzzy" Henry, Jack Randall, and the like. These were primarily western stars of the 1930's and were replaced by such sidestreet names as those of Gene Autry, Roy Rogers, Eddie Dean, Lash Larue, Sunset Carson and others, all of whom endeavored to keep alive the tradition of the western "programmer" in the periods of the 1940's and 1950's, when such films probably would have perished at the hands of many of the players of the 1930's.*

But regardless of the player who assayed the leading roles, the production which resulted usually was produced on one of the many western "sets" which were capable of presenting a creditable imitation of the "old west", among them Victorville, Lone Pine, Monogram Ranch, and so on. These locations did not often

present the kind of breathtaking beauty which John Ford included in such films as *Stage Coach* (which was filmed largely in Monument Valley, Utah) but did give a simulation of the old west, nonetheless.

These authentic backgrounds provided Poverty Row producers settings which were often far more convincing to film audiences than were the back lot sets of Twentieth Century-Fox or Warner Brothers — or even at the small independent film outfits, some of whose interior sets were crowded, simple, ersatz representations of a New York City street scene, or of an ocean liner. It was a big world reduced to an inexpensive microcosm.

Of the two motion picture types which were so much a staple on Poverty Row, the western is the more appealing, so beautifully simplistic in story style that its popularity over the years has been nothing short of amazing. There is a saying that "the movies first real film* was a western, and its final one will be, too."

Down through the years, hundreds of "oaters," as the film reviewers once termed westerns, have been ground out from a very limited number of plot situations, basically involving a hero who is confronted with some kind of evil, i.e., the dishonest banker, the bandit gang, the crooked politician, the scheming land baron, and so on. Of course, the plot is unimportant. Action is the theme, and the pitting of good against evil is the *raison d'etre*.

It would seem to be a simple and repetitive plot world, that of the

---

*Some of this number appeared in the so-called "trio westerns" in which three former western stars made up a team.

*The saying here is making reference to the Edison Company's *The Great Train Robbery* (1930) which was made in what were then the wilds of New Jersey, but was a western film.

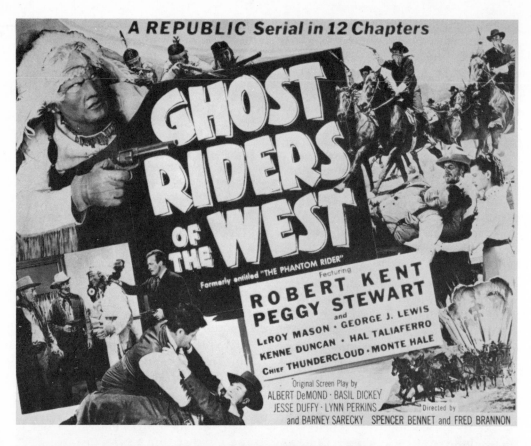

A REPUBLIC Serial in 12 Chapters

GHOST RIDERS OF THE WEST

Formerly entitled "THE PHANTOM RIDER"

Featuring

ROBERT KENT
PEGGY STEWART

and

LeROY MASON · GEORGE J. LEWIS
KENNE DUNCAN · HAL TALIAFERRO
Chief THUNDERCLOUD · MONTE HALE

Original Screen Play by
ALBERT DeMOND · BASIL DICKEY
JESSE DUFFY · LYNN PERKINS   Directed by
and BARNEY SARECKY   SPENCER BENNET and FRED BRANNON

Adventures of FRANK and JESSE JAMES

A RE-RELEASE

featuring

CLAYTON MOORE
STEVE DARRELL
NOEL NEILL
GEORGE J. LEWIS

Directed by FRED BRANNON and YAKIMA CANUTT
ORIGINAL SCREEN PLAY BY FRANKLIN ADREON ···
BASIL DICKEY ··· SOL SHOR

A
REPUBLIC
SERIAL IN **13** CHAPTERS

Chapter 2.   THE HIDDEN WITNESS

The advertising for all the Republic serials on these pages discloses how that studio often re-issued its chapter plays under names other than those employed by the original releases. Like Columbia, and others, Republic made a practice of such "re-issued" under false colors. [Photo by courtesy of Jack Jardine]

Formerly entitled "SECRET SERVICE in DARKEST AFRICA"

STARRING
ROD CAMERON
JOAN MARSH
WITH Duncan **RENALDO** Lionel **ROYCE**

Associate Producer W. J. O'SULLIVAN
Directed by SPENCER BENNET
A REPUBLIC SERIAL • 15 CHAPTERS

western. But even the great William Shakespeare gave little heed to the actual plots he used. (He revered character more than plot, with the result that many of his plots were conveniently "lifted" from other sources, as has been traced by scholars).

Part of the timeless appeal which the western has for audiences all over the world, is in their locale, which is rustic, large and challenging. Against such a background, players who are clad in

romantic garb play out their easily predictable tales, most of the stories glorified morality plays, much more acceptable to audiences as westerns than were the old morality plays which once were trucked about on wagons in "merrie" England.

Virtually the same plot elements found in the western carried over to the serial — with the important difference being that each serial possessed a group of moments of rising action occurring in the final moments of each episode, and not concluded until the start of the ensuing chapter. That, after all, was the basic "gimmick" of the latter-day serial picture.

The very limitations of the serials and westerns of Poverty Row gave rise to some of the area's brightest most interesting moments, imaginatively photographed by cameramen who had little time to study camera angles or lighting for each production.

Like the western film genre, the motion picture serial was well represented within the group of products from Poverty Row. Two firms Republic and Mascot, eventually turned out 97

A scene from **Custer's Last Stand** *[Stage and Screen Productions, 1936]. It is difficult to understand how such a slow-moving serial could have been fashioned from a theme involving "cowboys and Indians"; however, it was true in the case of this chapter play. Shown in his Indian regalia is Rex Lease. [Photo courtesy of Jan Barfoed]*

full chapter plays, released between 1927 and 1955.*

Even when the prospects for serials were good, as in the 1930's and 1940's, such films were shot at breakneck speed. Mascot Pictures, for example, shot a total of 24 thousand feet of edited film in just twenty-one working days!

Most of the Saturday matinee audience came to recognize serial

*The major studios were largely represented in this area of film making by Universal and Columbia, both of whom made serials less "satisfying" than the offerings of independent production entities, particularly Republic.

One of the most famous of the more than half a hundred serials which bore the Republic label, **The Lone Ranger** was released in 1938. Shown here are Lee Powell, Hal Taliaferro [Wally Wales], Lane Chandler, Bruce Bennett [Herman Brix] and George Montgomery. [Photo courtesy of Jan Barfoed]

Republic's serial offerings remained of the highest order in 1944, when the company offered **Zorro's Black Whip**. Shown here are John Merton, George Lewis and Hal Taliaferro [Wally Wales]. [Photo courtesy of Jan Barfoed]

heroes and heroines who were barely known, if at all recognizable, to those persons who frequented the large downtown theatres — players such as Ray "Crash" Corrigan, Ralph Byrd, Dick Purcell, Kay Aldridge, Lorna Gray, and Clayton Moore.

The history of the episode film had begun long before the "talking film era", in fact, in the year 1912* and finally extended to 1956, with the release of the Columbia serial, *Blazing the Overland Trail.* In that span of less than fifty years, serial production totalled about 231 pictures in sound versions, about 350 in silent films, for an approximate total of 581. It is not a terribly large output, but it was sufficient to establish the "cliff hanger" as a very popular part of the cinema. So the producers of Poverty Row serials were in effect, donning the mantle of a well-worn garment from what had once been a very profitable portion of the total film output per year — an era which created such stars as Pearl White, Helen Holmes, Elmo Lincoln, and many others.

In addition to Republic (and earlier, Mascot Pictures) a scant number of other independent film makers carried on the tradition just after the coming of the sound picture. Ben Wilson released the Wally Wales serial *Voice From the Sky* in 1930. Wales became better known as Hal Taliaferro, and under that name was a "heavy" in the casts of many pictures. Syndicate Pictures issued one titled, *Mystery Trooper* in 1931. Then sensing the boxoffice appeal in the Boy Scouts emblem, First Division came forth with a 1934 release titled, *Young Eagles. Queen of the Jungle,* a 12-

---

*The first American chapter play was a film called *What Happened to Mary?,* released in the summer of 1912 by the Edison Company.

episode offering which featured Reed Howes, came from Screen Attractions in 1935.

A small organization whose name seemed to embrace an impressive world, Stage and Screen Productions, offered the serials, *Custer's Last Stand, The Clutching Hand* and *The Black Coin,* all in 1936. Sam Katzman, another busy independent, presented the genre with two plays, *Shadow of Chinatown* with Bela Lugosi and *Blake of Scotland Yard* with Ralph Byrd, the pictures having been made in 1936 and 1937 respectively, and both of which Katzman issued under his Victory label.

The wonder of it is that small studios bothered to produce such chapter plays, for the rentals of each chapter brought in only about five dollars per theatre at most, while feature pictures brought in three times as much per showing and tied up personnel over a shorter time in their creation.

Monogram Pictures apparently felt that serials were hardly worth the effort. For example, they made no such films in their entire history, which is all the more surprising when one considers that the firm was organized by W. Ray Johnston, whose Rayart Company had produced so many serials in the silent film era.

During the silent picture era, Johnston's Rayart label had issued Elmo Lincoln in *King of the Jungle,* a 10-chapter serial (1927) as well as Ben Alexander in *Fighting for Fame* (1927), Herbert Rawlinson in *Trooper 77* (1926), *Scotty of the Scouts* (1926) which starred Herbert Rawlinson, *Phantom Police* (1926) another serial in which Rawlinson starred, *Mystery Pilot* (1926) with Rex Lease, *Secret Service Saunders* (1925) with Richard Holt, *The Flame Fighter* (1925) which again starred Herbert

Tom Mix's final screen appearance was in this 1935 Mascot serial, **The Miracle Rider**. A 15-chapter offering, the film was one of Mascot's final serials before the firm merged with Republic. [Photo courtesy of Jan Barfoed]

Rawlinson and *Battling Brewster* (1924) with Franklyn Farnum. So Johnston was well aware of the chapter play long before Monogram was born. In fact, Johnston was earlier a treasurer for Syndicate Film Company when they made the serial success of 1914. Yet, when Monogram came into being, it shied away from the chapter play, leaving that type of entertainment to Republic and to a handful of others.

Since the birth of that type of film, it underwent severe audience changes, it is true. In the World War I period, for example, such films attracted an adult audience to theatres, including a large following of women. Story lines were often published in newspapers and magazines which had largely an adult readership which helped to whet the appetites for the film.

By the time of talking picture popularity, however, the motion picture serial had become a "Saturday matinee" type of film, catering largely to children and to lovers of action fare. By that era, the casts of serials had women playing only incidental roles, for "talkie" pictures (serials) catered primarily to youthful audiences. A few "serial queens" developed in Republic's serials of the 1930's and 1940's, chiefly Frances Gifford and Kay Aldridge, but no female star of sound pictures ever seriously rivaled their male counterparts. For that reason, the female characters in serials were often largely unknown actresses, with few of them going beyond the serial and most disappearing completely as players once the chapter play was a thing of the past. (Kathlyn Williams and Pearl White were phenomena of a time when continued films drew a more adult trade to the theatre).

Most of the sound-era serials came from a handful of film studios and directors. Directors such as Spencer Gordon Bennet, John English, William Witney, B. Reeves, Breezy Eason, and a handful of others were responsible for a large percentage of the chapter plays. Only recently Bennet told the author of this book why the coterie of serial directors was so small. "A good director of regular features and westerns would be totally lost in working on serials. Chapter plays were entirely different. They were made by a system, and on budgets, which called for absolute economy of shooting time and expenditures."

The surprising thing about the really well-made serials of Poverty Row — for instance, those of Republic or Mascot — is that they provide a remarkably large number of backgrounds, and many action scenes which required careful staging as well as much breathtaking stunt work by such stuntmen as David Sharpe, Dick Talmadge and his brothers, (The Masettis), Cliff Lyons, Yakima Canutt, and others, including occasional superb miniatures by the Lydeckers, or one of the other firms of that time.

Yet, even when the popularity of the motion picture serial was relatively good, as in the 1930's and 1940's, such films were shot at breakneck speed. After all, each was a series of related short subjects, and as such, brought the studios which made them only a few dollars rental per episode per theatre, as stated earlier in this volume.

They were pulse-quickening entertainment. A form of screen mayhem that is usually overlooked by those film historians who seek only to cover that portion of cinema history which those historians regard as "artistic." Unfortunately, the rough-and-tumble of the serials and westerns does not often appeal to those who write film histories.

The serials were produced on infinitesimal budgets per foot of completed picture, one 15-chapter serial being more than five hours in length, which would be well above the running time of the famous picture *Gone With the Wind*.

"We shot those serials in the early days on a six day work week, dawn to dusk," said director Spencer Gordon Bennet, "not five days a week, nor at the present one of just four days."

The brevity of the shooting schedule for the serials, which was also true of westerns, was occasioned by budgetary requirements more than by the actual needs of the theatres themselves. Once a production was undertaken, it behooved the small producer to complete the picture quickly and at the lowest possible cost in order to get a rapid return, a maximum return on his investment.

"Above all else, you must remember that we produced pictures which were just grist for the producer's money mill," director John English once explained. "The profit on a feature or western which cost fifteen thousand dollars or twenty thousand, might be only a couple or three thousand dollars. If you consider that, you'll understand why most independent producers pinched pennies, used standardized plots and streamlined production methods. It was dollars and cents, that's all.

"Whether a director was turning out serials, westerns, or features, the independent director was always accountable to the financial department moreso than was the director at M-G-M, Paramount, or any other of the major firms."

The situation which John English outlined was a seemingly insurmountable one for the film artisan, but it was a climate which at least did not seriously hamper those film makers who chose to assay the serial and the western of the two decades we have chosen to cover.

*Pictured above is a lobby card describing the **BLAKE OF SCOTLAND YARD** serial—starring Ralph Byrd in 15 thrilling chapters.*

Locations

LIKE the spokes of a wheel, the many "locations" which Poverty Row film producers used were webbed about Los Angeles, all of them visited by film crews and film players who were employed by independent film producers.

Did a producer from Poverty Row want a harbor for use in his next film? San Pedro was very convenient to get to and for filming.

How about some exciting automobile chase scenes on lonely, tortuous roads? They could easily be obtained along the confines of winding, wild Mulholland Drive, just to the north of Hollywood.

And ranches? Ah-h there too, the area abounded. Lone Pine, to the north of town. Hemet, to the south and east. Newhall to the north and west. And such other locales as Victorville, Chatsworth, and Vasquez Rocks, too. All within easy distance of Hollywood — and getting easier to reach by the time World War II got underway, though nonetheless, each appearing primitive, remote, and each one photogenic.

To the east of Hollywood were the apparently tractless desert areas which abounded in scenes so empty in their vastness, as expressed in Mascot's serial *The Three Musketeers;* while to the north, the "snow country" of the upper regions of San Fernando, as used in so many James Oliver Curwood films. Any type of locale was easily conjured up within just a few hours drive of Hollywood — as the producers of Poverty Row knew full well.

Film producer Edward Finney recalls how such location shooting had the fun of a camping trip and the practicality of an industrial branch office. "The area around what we later called 'Corriganville' was convenient and inviting; besides, it possessed a 'western street' in which many of the buildings could actually be used for sleeping quarters for members of the cast and crew."

Such functionality became increasingly the keynote, as World War II ended and money-saving ideas a more integral part of Poverty Row procedures, and which could provide those Poverty Row filmers that remained with such diverse views as that of an artificial lake, the vastness of ranch country and the man-made crudeness of a frontier town.

In the era when Poverty Row was a very real force among Hollywood film makers, the area around Lone Pine, California, was an important one. Lone Pine is on the north end of a dry lake bed known as Owens Lake. Moreover, the town is just 125 miles from Hollywood, almost due north of the film capital. Sparsely settled in what was a "frontier" area of California in the 1920's and 1930's, it was the gateway to the famous Panamint Range of peaks —

and to Death Valley. It remains, all in all, both an historic and a picturesque area, deservedly well chosen by film makers of Hollywood in general and by the filmers who were numbered among Poverty Row's citizens.

For those production chieftains of the Gower Gulch area of Hollywood who felt that their films warranted the additional mileage, numerous unspoiled western vistas as those to be found in Utah, Arizona, and Wyoming were but a few hours train ride from Hollywood. After all, the expression, "A rock is a rock, a tree is a tree — shoot the scene in Griffith Park", may or may not have originated with one of the Stern Brothers down on Poverty Row, but the prevailing credo among the Gower Gulch production men definitely was that their production personnel should range far and wide in the making of features and serials — but only as the budget allowed, of course.

Not always did such far-ranging philosophy result in Poverty Row epics, however. "In June of 1938, we were hit by one of the worst floods in California history," producer Edward Finney recalls. "At the time, I was in production of an outdoor film. It was a terrible setback, let me tell you.   "Worst of all, I was committed to all my stars, all my crew. What a dilemma for a producer!

"In a most un-California-like manner, we shot in a large garage at Newhall Ranch, opening the back doors to give the illusion of the outdoors, and to sort of 'fool the camera' so to speak. With some 'stock footage' added to the finished film to lend the feeling of bigness to the finished material. I managed to turn out a quite satisfactory screen version of The Pioneers, James Fenimore Cooper's classic which is one of that author's "Leatherstocking Tales."

Most of the time, however, film companies were more fortunate than Mr. Finney's crew was. Regardless of the location that film producers required, a California version could usually be found near Hollywood. For example, the mechanical, mysterious background of the oil field existed almost in Hollywood's back yard — in Los Angeles itself. The refineries, too, were not much farther off (as Republic Pictures crews discovered to film viewer's awe).

Not far from that man-made conglomerate of steel tanks and piping, across a few miles of ocean, was a series of "South Sea Islands" which producers both small and large used repeatedly in their pictures. The property, known the world over as Catalina and its neighboring islands, was hardly recognizable by film audiences when the spits of land doubled for the islands of the South Seas.

Few of the Poverty Row producers found it necessary to travel far afield for their film backgrounds, although a few squandered production dollars on location scenes made in Monument Valley, Arizona, or in some alluring place in Utah, Wyoming or the like.

In most cases, however, the producers of "B" films were quite satisfied with the settings in and near Los Angeles, either those locales which were used over and over as motion picture sets, or were occasionally so favored.

Of the two clans which existed in Hollywood — the major production outfits and the independent film makers — it was by far the smaller firms who exploited the "location scenes" for their pictures. And it is an important factor in adding realism to the Poverty Row output of the 1930's and 1940's.

Today, most of the early "locations" once favored by Hollywood are just names, not even on a map — or are nearly forgotten pieces of California landscape. Vasquez Rocks, Iverson's Ranch, Corriganville, the Monogram Ranch, Calabasas, Chatsworth, Hemet, and other names of places once providing Poverty Row with the backgrounds which made their films scenic, vast and appealing, are now gone, or nearly so.

Some of the locations belonged once to some film studio, or to someone who made a good part of his annual income from renting his "location," as did film player Ray "Crash" Corrigan with his once famous "Corriganville" — now one of the holdings of comedian Bob Hope — and which originally cost Corrigan only about a tenth of the $800,-000 he resold it for after World War II.

"It was a good investment for Corrigan to have made," one picture producer said not long ago, "and any set which a producer erected out at Corrigan's place became a permanent one on the property. As a result, Corriganville was constantly enlarging." It was not only a case of good business. It was one very valid reason why film audiences did not become aware of how often they were actually viewing the same backgrounds!

"We had a limitless number of locations in and close to Hollywood," commented one cameraman recently, "but we had certain ones we favored, usually because we were familiar with them, and thus knowing they'd be right when we got out on the site."

For all of Hollywood's attempts to give motion picture audiences the same kind of familiarity, the "on location" scenes have gone into film history with a surprisingly diverse appearance.

Location shooting north of Hollywood. A scene from one of Ken Maynard's numerous pictures.

Other Dwellers
Of Poverty Row

WHEN the sound picture craze hit Hollywood, it brought forth a host of small producers who were willing to undertake the production of "talking pictures" and, more specifically, films of a nature which would subjugate sound to action, thus tailoring such pictures to those theatres which catered to audiences which loved action above all else.

If one recites a list of such producers, the Weiss Brothers are always prominent. Max, Louis and Adolph Weiss entered film production in the early 1920's, using money the brothers had made in the ownership of the Welsbach Lamp and Fixture Store in New York City, which in turn had led the brothers into phonograph sales, and finally to ownership of a theatre at New York's Avenue A and 4th Street. That theatre eventually became a small chain of movie houses and moreover, convinced them that there were vast profits to be made in film production.

Accordingly, the brothers entered production in 1922 with a feature called *After Six Days,* soon after which the brothers became full time dwellers of Hollywood's Poverty Row, and producers of a good many action films and serials. These kept the firm active as long as there was an independent film market, accepting many of these productions which were offered as Stage and Screen Productions and as Artcraft Productions.

Close on the heels of the Weiss Brothers, paternally trod another New Yorker, Sam Katzman, a producer who presented his films to theatres under a variety of labels, sometimes distributing the finished product himself, but more often offering it through some larger distribution setup. In recent years, Katzman has stayed with the Columbia label. Earlier, he had been distributing, often through Monogram, a part of his productions called "Four Bell Productions" or "Banner Productions" which had produced several *East Side Kids* films with essentially the same players who came to later fame at Monogram as "The Bowery Boys" but under another producer.

Before his days of association with the Monogram label, however, Katzman had free-lanced under the name of Victory Pictures, which in the mid-1930's had produced a number of features made from stories authored by Peter B. Kyne, and the serials, *Blake of Scotland Yard* and *Shadow of Chinatown.*

A detailed and really accurate study of the production figures along Poverty Row would be incomplete without the name of C. C. Burr, the Brooklyn-born producer who went from a position as a newspaper reporter to an advertising manager for Paramount Pictures, and finally into film production in the 1920's. A pioneer producer of Monogram releases, Burr contracted in 1935 and

*Westerns which talked were still something of a novelty in 1931 when Big Four Pictures made **Riders of the Cactus** with Wally Wales [Hal Taliaferro] and Tete Brady. [Photo courtesy of Jan Barfoed]*

1936 with Puritan Pictures to do a series of melodramas. Puritan, incidentally, did only a few pictures, all of them in the two years that Burr was associated with the firm. *Skybound, Kentucky Blue Streak, Man From Guntown, Outlaw Deputy,* and *Rip Roaring Riley* (all in 1935) and *Rogue's Tavern, Roaring Guns, Border Cavallero, I'll Name the Murderer* and *Lightnin' Bill Carson* (all in 1936) with the titles indicative of the low cost locales of Puritan Pictures, were all that were produced. Many of these starred the dependable western player Tim McCoy, whose career in films — usually in westerns — began soon after World War I and continued into the 1960's. Like Bob Steele and Johnny Mack Brown, Tim McCoy was a continuing "star" of Poverty Row productions.

Another name prominent among Poverty Row producers was A. W. Hackel, whose mid-1930 releases were handled by "leading independent film exchanges" as his advertising described it. Hackel, who called his firm Supreme Pictures Corporation, produced primarily western pictures, a large number of which starred Bob Steele and some which featured Johnny Mack Brown.

During the period from 1932 through 1935, another small Poverty Row outfit called Mayfair Pictures Corporation turned out a rather large handful of action features which, while not embracing any westerns, are nonetheless worthwhile recounting because Mayfair's films were so titled as to indicate the types of pictures they were. On the lower half of a double feature program of the period, pictures such as *Alimony Madness, Riot Squad, Oil Raider, Midnight Warning* or *Fighting Rookie* would usually find an acceptable spot. These pictures, and seventeen more of similar content, were the total output of Mayfair, which like Chesterfield, Ambassador-Conn, and other Small "action film studios" of the thirties counted their profits excellent if each picture was able to make a few thousand dollars per picture.

John English, then a film editor and later director for Ambassador-Conn, once recalled, "On Poverty Row, there were many producers who in the 1930's were quite satisfied to make a profit of only three or four thousand dollars per picture, believe it or not." Probably Mayfair was no exception.

Such producers as those outlined here often did not have studio facilities of their own, but instead based their operations within a mere office building. More often, they rented office space within one of the large lots of the "rental stages" at which time they would also rent a sound stage or two for

actual production of a film.

The "rental stages" most popular in the 1930's included those of RKO Pathe at Culver City, the old Talisman Studio on Sunset Boulevard, General Service Studios at 6625 Romaine Street, and to a lesser degree the Tec-Art Studios, Prudential Studios and the Larry Darmour Studios. Other small rental stages also were maintained for a time by International Film Corporation, and by a firm which called its operation at 6117 Sunset — Television Studios — a prophetic and ironic sort of mid-1930 title for a film outfit!

Such firms afforded Poverty Row film makers a host of well-equipped sound stages to which any might turn when in

Bernard B. Ray's little Reliable Pictures offered this western, **Coyote Trails**, *[1935]. Shown with Tyler is sidekick Ben Corbett. [Photo courtesy of Jan Barfoed]*

need of such facilities, and eliminated the need for small producers to maintain such expensive installations. For the bulk of the features which were made on Poverty Row — especially in the period of the 1930's — "location shooting" comprised the bulk of the scenes which were made.

Maurice H. Conn, for instance, maintained his headquarters at the Talisman Studios, on Sunset Boulevard. By means of three different releasing labels — Ambassador-Conn Pictures, Conn Pictures and Melody Pictures Corporation — this busy young producer managed the release of a great many features which were handled through "states right" film exchanges based in thirteen key cities around the United States and which extended to various foreign countries, as well.

For a time, Conn released a series of "Northwest Mountie" films, which starred Ken Maynard's younger brother Kermit, and another action film series jointly starring Kane Richmond and juvenile star Frankie Darro.

Conn had begun his film production work with Nat Levine whose Mascot Pictures were indeed a good proving ground for ambitious newcomers!

This diversity of independent production and producers — most of them buried grandiosely behind logos which were deliberately impressive — came to include a variety of production firms, which eventually included Big 4 Pictures, Syndicate Pictures, Chesterfield Motion Pictures, Majestic and many more, particularly during the early "talking picture" era, just prior to World War II.

*Reliable Pictures turned out western offerings, although the lifespan of the little company was but brief. This is a scene from one of Reliable's 1935 offerings, **Wolf Riders**. Shown here in the scene are Lillian Gilmore, Jack Perrin and Lafe McKee. [Photo courtesy of Jan Barfoed]*

Scene from Mascot's 1934 feature **Crimson Romance**. At left is "the man you love to hate," Erich von Stroheim. With him is Ben Lyon and Hardie Albright.

Erich von Stroheim with Wera Engels from the movie **Fugitive Road** [1934] a production of Invincible films.

This 1937 Spectrum picture, **Melody of the Plains**, was one of several of the Fred Scott "singing westerns" some of which were produced for Spectrum by comedian Stan Laurel. Shown above are Al St. John, Billy Lenhart and Fred Scott. [Photo courtesy of Jan Barfoed]

Skull and Crown in which Jack Mulhall starred, was one of Bernard B. Ray's Reliable Picture releases of the 1930's and one of countless "Poverty Row" productions in which Rin-Tin-Tin, Jr. starred [but who is unfortunately, not pictured here].

Kermit Maynard appeared in a series of films made by Maurice Conn's Ambassador Pictures, such as this 1937 one, **Rough Riding Rhythm.** Shown with Maynard is Ralph Peters. [Photo courtesy of Jan Barfoed]

As a sequel to the company's 1945 feature **Wildfire**, which had featured Bob Steele, Screen Guild released **Return of Wildfire** [1948] in which the important roles went to [left to right] Richard Arlen, Patricia Morrison, Mary Beth Hughes and Chris Pin Martin. [Photo courtesy of Robert L. Lippert]

Robert Lowery and Ken Curtis were the featured players in the Lippert feature **Call of the Forest** [1949]. The boy is producer Edward Finney's young son. [Photo courtesy of Robert L. Lippert]

In upgrading the casts and production values of its releases, Lippert Pictures co-featured Vincent Price and Ellen Drew in **Baron of Arizona** [1950], based on a factual story of the old west. [Photo courtesy of Robert L. Lippert]

It seemed anachronistic to announce entry into independent film production in 1946, for by then, the shadow of television was darkening the skies of Hollywood. Nonetheless, that was the year that the organization of Screen Guild was announced. Moreover, before the year was out, the new firm had released its initial Cinecolor feature offering *Wildfire* with Western player Bob Steele (released in 1945, it was Screen Guild's only offering that year). The picture was made earlier by Action Pictures, which producer Robert L. Lippert headed.

Spearheading the new firm were John J. Jones, who was named president of the organization, and Robert L. Lippert, who was designated as vice president. Of the two officials however, it was Lippert who eventually reigned supreme, and indeed, reorganized and renamed the company Lippert Pictures, Incorporated. Prior to his association with Screen Guild, Lippert had operated a film production unit known as Action Pictures, Incorporated. Primarily though, Lippert's activities had centered around a theatre circuit which included about sixty theatres in Southern Oregon and in California. From that, he had branched into production, with the results that we are examining.

The Screen Guild name was used until the Spring of 1949 at which time all releases were designated as those of Lippert Pictures, Inc. At first, the Lippert features were of the same ilk with the Screen Guild releases. By the early 1950's however, a few bigger "names" entered Lippert's films and production values were improved. During the combined histories of Screen Guild and Lippert Pictures, the firms offered several features in Cinecolor, *Wildfire, God's Country* and *Scared to Death* and a handful of films made with cameras which were equipped with the "Gurutsa lens," a device which simulated a three-dimensional screen image by means of separately focusing the foreground and background of a scene. Incidently, Screen Guild/Lippert were the only studios to experiment with the device.

There was no Screen Guild or Lippert Studio as such. Instead, rental stages were utilized, first at Nassour Brothers and even smaller stage rental buildings, and in 1959 at Republic Studios. Favorite "location scenes" for Lippert features were filmed at the Ray Corrigan Ranch at Chatsworth, California.

After the designation Lippert Pictures replaced Screen Guild's*, the firm made or distributed 130 features, all between 1948 and 1955. Not long ago, Lippert glanced back across the production history of the two firms, pointing out seven features which he considered to be "major" offerings, *Baron of Arizona* (featuring Vincent Price), *Rocket Ship X-M* (with Lloyd Bridges), *I Shot Jesse James* (starring Preston Foster) and such post-1950 pictures as *Hell Gate* (featuring Sterling Hayden), *Little Big Horn* (with John Ireland), *Sins of Jezebel* (with Paulette Goddard) and Sam Fuller's production titled *Steel Helmet*.

When television reduced motion picture theatre attendance, and eliminated many of those theatres which presented double feature programs, most of the independent producers ceased production. In 1956, Robert L.

Rocket Ship X-M was something of a deluxe feature for Lippert Pictures. The cast of the picture was good, consisting as it did of [left to right] Noah Beery, Jr., Hugh O'Brien, Osa Massen and Lloyd Bridges. [Photo courtesy of Robert L. Lippert]

Lippert formed a new film organization called Regal Films, releasing its product through 20th Century-Fox. Eventually, Regal produced 180 pictures, a remarkable record when one considers the slump which Hollywood was in at the time. One of the wiser, luckier producers of the many who inhabited the independent orbit, Robert L. Lippert profited by his production activities, which eventually spanned better than two decades. When it was ended, he returned to San Francisco, and to his activities as a theatre operator, the Hollywood segment of his life gracefully ended.

It is impossible to give detailed accounts of the many other producing and distributing firms which made up the mythical Hollywood area called Poverty Row. Indeed, it is not necessary to do so. Some were merely distribution firms, as with Capital Film Exchange of New York City, which distributed the pictures of Majestic, Mascot and other outfits, and represented those companies in the New York area. Others, like DuWorld, specialized in film imports, which were only marginally acceptable to U. S. audiences. Firms, such as Conquest Pictures Company, offered largely, feature documentaries, another marginally profitable field of the pre-World War II era.

There was also the New York based firm called Empire Film Distributors, which offered primarily the motion pictures made by Mayfair, and a series of cheap westerns which starred Lane Chandler.

World Wide released **Man From Hell's Edges** which starred Bob Steele [right]. This Poverty Row production outfit eventually released its product through Fox. [Photo courtesy of Jan Barfoed]

A reproduction of one of the lobby cards for a Maynard western of the mid-1930's. Colony was a small production outfit which occupied an inconspicuous corner of Poverty Row and which survived but a short time. [Photo from the author's collection]

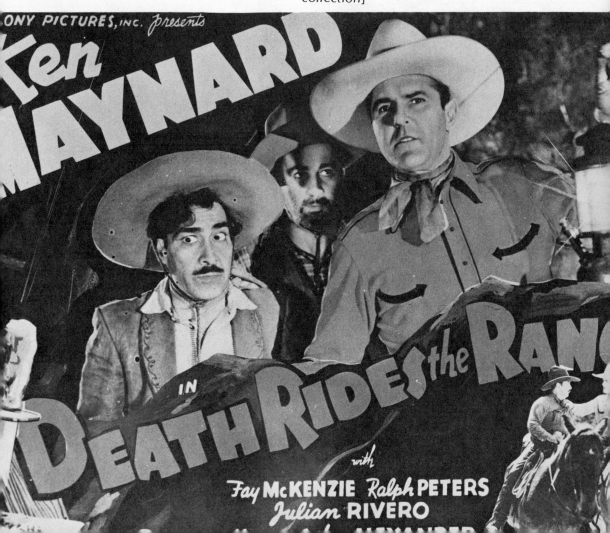

ONY PICTURES, INC. *presents*

KEN MAYNARD

IN DEATH RIDES THE RANGE

with

Fay McKENZIE Ralph PETERS

Julian RIVERO

Harry Carey was a New Yorker. However, he rode to screen fame as a cowboy, making numerous western appearances throughout the 1930's and to a lesser extent, in the 1940's. Still later, he carved another screen career as a character actor, his last screen appearance being in such a role as in the feature by Walt Disney, **So Dear to My Heart**. He appeared in the 1930's and 1940's in features and serials made by Big 4, Mascot and Monogram along with Republic. [Photo from author's collection]

While these distribution names and several others added confusion to the production history of features and allied subjects, the companies made available the products of Poverty Row and as such were a necessary part of its history. All of it came about because motion picture audiences were vast at the time, demanding thousands of feet of film which the eight "major" studios could not effectively supply.

It is how, after all, Poverty Row came into being, and how the largest of its ranks — Republic Pictures — became as profitable. It is why it all ended after World War II, when its public would no longer pay to see those films which they could see for nothing on television.

Sic Transit Gloria!

Mr. Boggs Steps Out *was originally to be titled* **Mr. Boggs Buys a Barrel.** *Produced by Ben Pivar from a script inspired by some Clarence Budington Kelland short stories which appeared in Saturday Evening Post, the film starred Stuart Erwin and Helen Chandler [shown above].*

The Old Order Changeth

A mere twenty years isn't long in the recorded history of man, it's true. Two decades isn't even a third of the life span of the average person. But just that amount of time was sufficient to embrace some important events in American history, and of world events. The pair of decades, 1930 to 1950, then, were filled practically to the minute with events of truly great import.

Historically, they were eras of a great global economic crisis (which today is only dimly recalled to mind), as well as a widespread and terrible world war. It opened with the chugging of the Model A Ford and closed with the sleekness of cars with V-8 engines encapsuled in bullet-shaped shells capable of smoothly roaring along vast complexes of efficient highways which had only been hinted at for the Model A world which existed twenty years before.

The motion pictures from Hollywood during these hectic decades were but nitrate reflections of events and dreams which occupied a very large proportion of the world as it existed and changed at that time.

As for the manner in which these events — cinematic and otherwise— affected the author of this work, the reader must realize that the book was empirically grounded in the theatres of Saginaw, Michigan, a city which, prior to World War II, consisted of some 67 thousand persons, and nearly two dozen movie houses, most of which presented many of the independently-made films of Hollywood.

This microcosm contained, during the halcyon movie years of 1936-1937, such cinema palaces as the Temple, a vast mausoleum-like structure which offered moviegoers such things as ushers in uniform, potted plants in the lobby and other "Roxy" touches. Of the dozen or so other Saginaw theatres which at that time were viable customers for products of the less affluent of Hollywood producers, most were grimy little copies of small theatres in all parts of the world.

One such survivor of the nickelodeon of silent film days was the Northside, a 300-seat cinema which started in the silent era (with an automatic piano near the small silver screen) and prospered during World War II as an all-night "grind house" which served defense plant workers. The theatre so survived until the competition of television finally crushed it, as it did so many other "marginal" theatre operations.

Until that happened, though, the Northside operated virtually without shutting down for longer than necessary to clean the place — or to make it as tidy as necessary, which was none too fastidious, you may be sure. In all that time, its tiny projection booth was equipped with nothing better than a pair of ancient pre-talkie era Powers 6-B Projection machines on which (when "talkies" arrived) hung the necessary apparatus for reproducing "sound on film."

Its small auditorium was starkly functional, its seats fitting to the ana-chronistic facade of the theatre, which sported a nearly solid semi-circle of glass poster display cases, lighted bril-liantly, if starkly, with lamps along three chipping archways. The dreams to be conjured up by one's attendance at such a film hall existed strictly within the darkened auditorium, most specifically, being conjured from some outlandish Hollywood cowboy as he crossed the aluminum-surfaced screen, his six-guns roaring, calling theatre-wide attention to the smudged canvas, and to the animate dreams thrown thereon.

Prior to the mid-point in World War II, theatres such as the Northside were very much a portion of the indoor theatres of the world, effectively cater-ing to a cinema audience which for the most part had not heard of the drive-in movie,* and who only had dreamed of the phenomenal gadgetry involved in television.

The Northside and its numerous brethren existed in all parts of the United States, and were consciously or unconsciously reproduced throughout the world — the Yank Theatre in Luxembourg and the Everyman's Theatre in London, being brothers

under their shabby skins with the Northside, Saginaw, Michigan. They were merely cinematic evidence of two decades of motion picture popularity.

These theatres existed within a duo of unlike decades which for film producers along Poverty Row saw vast changes as had the world at large. In the first decade, numerous small production companies had been optimistically created, few of which survived even that ten year period. The ensuing decade saw the emergence of a handful of independent film makers as the survivors of the hectic craze for estab-lishing film "studios." Their pro-ductions were often made on briefly rented stages, their fanciful trademarks often hinting at grandiose schemes for the same kind of fame and respect-ability which by that time was accorded Paramount, Warner Brothers, M-G-M, Columbia, RKO, United Artists, Twentieth Century-Fox, and Universal.

By the coming of 1940, the changes all along Gower Gulch were toward the consolidation of the independent film outfits into three production centers — Republic, Monogram and PRC. A fourth, smaller operation, emerged after World War II, in a label first called Screen Guild Pictures and later, Lippert Pictures. The company's uneasy toehold in Hollywood was too precarious, however, and the forces of television too imminent to give their film making activities a very long period. Independent film production had clearly changed, had become more expensive and vastly less interesting than it had been during the Depression Years and World War II.

In only two decades the entire film making pattern had changed sharply, even as had the audience tastes in screen entertainment. From the

---

*What is generally accepted as being the first drive-in movie theatre was build in New Jersey in 1939. As generally accepted popular enter-tainment, television did not make serious inroads into movie theatre attendance prior to 1953.

Depression years, during most of which the sheer novelty of movies that talked was sufficient, to the World War II years in which the screen constituted a never-never land conjuring up tales which came to organized, solid conclusions, the world audience came to witness a maturing cinema.

But in the post-war years, as one writer phrased it, the film studios "were ill-prepared for the revolution they faced. They had grown soft to the ready demand for their product, and suddenly found that people by the millions were staying home to watch television . . . " From a wartime peak production of 600 feature pictures annually, Hollywood found itself scarcely able to market half that number per year.

The small independent studios — the dwellers of Hollywood's Poverty Row — got what they could, financially, from the sudden rise of television, of course. Initially, the major studios shunned TV entirely, in the hope that they could somehow starve it. At the same time, however, producers and ex-producers of independent films dumped 16mm copies of their 1930 and 1940 era offerings into major TV outlets, making the films of Poverty Row available to a vast audience, only a portion of which had been seen when they were current fare in smaller theatres.

Eventually, the television networks dried up this market for the independent cinema, thus killing off even the memory of Poverty Row, its producers and stars. It was a sad electronic finish to an industry which at one time employed so many persons that it was among the major employers throughout America.

The Poverty Row film maker was, after all, but a shabby cousin of the diamond-studded "major producer," and together they were inundated by other forces within the entertainment and recreation world.

It was, as Alfred Lord Tennyson put it, a case where "the old order changeth, giving way to the new," an era which still is not completely gone.

Epilog

POVERTY Row is gone now.

The one-time populace of that mythical section of Hollywood has scattered. Many have passed away.

Those firms of Poverty Row which remain have retrenched in their operations. The studios of both Republic and Monogram have become television production facilities. PRC's (earlier Grand National's) studios have long since been razed. The old Tiffany lot still exists. Little else, however, remains to remind one of Poverty Row or its history.

The Poverty Row phase of Hollywood history parallels that of the major film studios, except that some of the majors have been able to keep alive their trademarks, though often only through television productions.

The canyons where once the cowboys from Gower Gulch rode triumphant, are seldom visited these days by camera crews. Indeed, many have been turned into housing developments or supermarkets and parking lots.

It is a small part of the world's history, a past that slipped by when most of us weren't looking. One day, there were ten million brilliant lights illuminating ten thousand and more American movie theatres. Then, almost in an impossible moment, they were gone. The ten million bulbs were forever dark, and with that Poverty Row put out its lights, too.

Alphabetical Index